21st-CENTURY ETIQUETTE

21st-CENTURY ETIQUETTE

Charlotte Ford's Guide to Manners for the Modern Age

Charlotte Ford
with Jacqueline deMontravel

The Lyons Press
Guilford, Connecticut
An imprint of The Globe Pequot Press

For my grandchildren
Charlotte, Callie, Alessandro & Annabelle

With deep love, affection and pride. With hope that this
can help guide you in the right direction.

I love you.

The Lyons Press is an imprint of The Globe Pequot Press.

Printed in the United States of America

10 9 8 7 6 5 4 3 2

Design by Compset, Inc.

Illustrations © 2001 Sally Mara Sturman

Library of Congress Cataloging-in-Publication Data

Ford, Charlotte, date.
    21st century etiquette: Charlotte Ford's guide to manners for the mod-
ern age/Charlotte Ford.
      p. cm.
    Includes index.
    ISBN 1-58574-337-2
    1. Etiquette. I. Title: Twenty-first century etiquette. II. Title.

BJ1853.F59 2001
395—dc21

2001038729

CONTENTS

Chapter III—Table Manners

Chapter IV—Dining Right

Chapter V—That's Entertaining

INTRODUCTION

*W*hat's the first thing that comes to mind when you hear the word "etiquette"? If you're thinking "stuffy," "dated," "snobbish," and "impractical," you're not alone. I, too, have been wondering if the courtly manners of centuries past are as constraining as the corsets that civil-minded ladies once wore. Nevertheless, at the dawn of the millennium, I presented myself with a new century resolution, to write my third etiquette book, one that is appropriate for today's times.

At first the writing process was cathartic—observing and then venting on my daily run-ins with bad behavior. I then rationalized practical solutions. While this was personally gratifying, it was through my communication with others on the subject of manners that I received the most encouragement. I was surprised to find that while the formal notion of etiquette does indeed seem to have gone the way of the dodo, many people from all backgrounds are mourning the loss in our society of good manners and basic civility. What they are longing for is simply a return to a more respectful world.

Imagine always hearing "Pardon" after someone jostles you in line at the movies or receiving a thank-you note from a friend you treated to lunch. It's a wonder to me that etiquette has acquired such an antiquated image since all of these simple acts of respect are what etiquette is really all about. Rather than approach it as a daunting set of uptight rules (and who really likes rules?), let's redefine etiquette as the kind gestures we show toward others throughout the day.

While today's society is experiencing changes as quickly as Microsoft can put out a new piece of software, human behavior is also evolving at twenty-first century speed. Once upon a time, personal sentiments were exchanged via formal, handwritten notes. The only place one heard a telephone ring was in the privacy of one's home or office. Flash forward to the new millennium where e-mail correspondence, cell phones, and the anonymity of the Internet has bred a somewhat more careless and certainly more rushed interaction between human beings. While technological advancements undoubtedly improve everyday activity, we seem to have lost something meaningful in our relationships with one another. It seems to me these cyber-times have made us forget who we are.

And it is not just technology that is changing us. New social customs and mores have crept into our lives over the past several decades. Everything from dress-down Fridays to single-parenting to single-sex marriages has thrown those old-fashioned, outdated notions of etiquette into a tizzy. We are left the daunting task, should we even bother to undertake it, of muddling through such confusing social situations on our own.

All is not lost, however. Before dot-com discourtesy becomes commonplace and before the new world order threatens to overwhelm us, a nod to manners can easily bring civility back into our busy lives. Like modern art displayed in a historic building, modern life and good manners can exist together with both practicality and grace.

My hope is that this guide to manners in the twenty-first century will serve as a road map to get us back on the track of good behavior. It is less an ironclad set of rules than a book of suggestions that will help put a bit of mutual respect and common civility back into the world.

CHAPTER 1

TAMING TECHNOLOGY

In the new century, high-tech gadgetry and the speed and efficiency of technology influences almost every aspect of our lives. All generations now use cell phones, e-mail, and the Internet. A close look at the modern family reveals that everyone is connected electronically in some way: Parents assist their children with homework on the family PC, grandparents are e-mailing their grandchildren. It's faster to get in touch with someone, it's faster to get your work done—so you would think. Take a moment to see how the advent of technological advancements has improved your lifestyle. If you're like me, all of this speed and advancement has actually created *less* time for simple pleasures. The greatest competitor of good manners may be the haste, speed, and unwieldy nature of the technology beast. Soon a well-written e-mail becomes a garbled note filled with errors; cell phones and call waiting invade your life with no consideration of those around you.

Let's face it, most of us take for granted how much trouble our communication devices can cause—infiltrating poor habits into all lifestyle situations. These very devices that bring us closer also keep us further away and make it easy for us to forget our manners. I have a friend who is constantly checking her e-mail when she visits for the weekend; I've also observed others bringing their laptops to their child's soccer game. Here we stand at the turn of the century hardly able to find the end of the workday. Rather than forfeit to a medium that has a computer chip for a brain, maintain human control by instituting social graces in a new age.

Electronic etiquette is an intriguing new territory for those who help set the standard of good behavior, and numerous new questions arise. What are the rules of etiquette with technology? May we fax an invitation? May we take our cell phones to a dinner party? May we leave a condolence message on an answering machine? How many times may we reasonably ask a friend to "hold" when call waiting beeps?

In negotiating each of these issues, there is one guiding principal to remember: The whole point of good manners is to respect other people's comfort and privacy so that they may be at ease. This applies to cell phones and e-mail just as surely as it applies to table manners.

Multitasking

Remember that guy from high school who could pat his belly, recite the alphabet, and tap his head all at once? That's what I imagine when I hear the word "multitasking." Multitasking is the catch phrase used to describe the act of performing several modern functions at once. For example, typing an e-mail to a friend while proofing a work memo as you call for a pizza. You could say that multitasking is a skill, kind of like juggling. I'd drop all of the balls at the first attempt. While it's a thrill to accomplish so much at once, keep in mind that it's important to perform each task well. Don't sacrifice proper grammar in an e-mail or incorrectly address a colleague in a memo because you were taking a phone call at the same time. If performing one task to completion before you begin another will cost you an extra five minutes, take the time. The extra effort will pay for itself in the long run when you don't have to go back and correct your embarrassing mistake.

E-tiquette

Providing instant conversation with family, friends, and business colleagues around the world, e-mail is perhaps one of the most useful and efficient inventions of modern times. Not only has e-mail revived the timeless art of correspondence, but it has also given us a new venue for a good dose of humor. I have received some of the best jokes electronically. I don't know where these jokes have been hiding, but a teaspoon of instant humor has certainly brightened many a dull day. However, e-mail can also be as addictive as the latest tabloid scandal.

The joke in the office is that people who are within plain sight of one another send e-mail messages instead of speaking. Business executives, grammar school kids, and people of all walks of life depend on their e-mail on a daily if not hourly basis. With such a powerful new tool in our lives, it's only natural that we've not yet gotten the hang of using it with proper respect. Like any other form of communication, there is a proper way to handle it. "E" is for etiquette in e-mail. Your friends and family will appreciate the effort you make, and good e-mail form will make professional matters more pleasant for all.

Think of the etiquette that governs e-mail as similar to the etiquette that governs written correspondence sent through the post. Always use a person's name in the initial salutation and sign off with, at the very least, your name. In more formal business correspondence you might consider including your title and your company's name, address, your direct phone number, and fax number, depending upon the recipient. A handy device is the signature line offered by most systems in which you can program all of your relevant contact information. Most e-mail systems include the date and the time of your message, so it's not necessary to include these in the body of the text. However, you should always reference a subject in the line provided and try to be as concise here as possible.

In the body of the text, be clear, succinct, and courteous in your comments. You don't have to prepare a formal document each time you send an e-mail, but certainly do not drop all the rules of grammar even in just a short note. Installing the spell check and grammar check on your e-mail will help avoid such errors.

If your e-mail is in response to one you received, reference the key topic in the subject bar and clue your correspondent in on the points to which you are responding. Some systems even allow you to copy text from the e-mail you received onto the e-mail you're sending so you can respond directly point by point.

Instant Messaging

Many Internet home pages and e-mail servers are equipped with "Instant Messaging" options. Since the purpose of instant messaging is to have a quick (usually social) conversation, you need not be so concerned with the formalities of e-mail. Omitting a salutation and close is allowed. Be careful, however, not to get too caught up in the informality of it all. Notably, instant messaging with friends while at the office is not a good idea. In some companies it's even forbidden. Spending professional time chatting with your friends through instant messaging is essentially the same as chatting on the phone all day—neither is appropriate during work hours.

Instant messaging is also an option on some mobile phones. It can be a great tool for when you're on a bus or in some other public place when a loud phone call can be distracting to those around you. However, just as you would with a cell phone, keep this feature turned off when you're out with friends, colleagues, etc.

Group E-mail/personal

Sending group e-mails is an efficient way to inform personal acquaintances of essential information—news that you are moving, of an engagement, the birth of a child, etc. However, it is wise to use the blind copy feature when addressing each recipient. Not everyone likes to have their private e-mail address—akin to a private telephone number—given out to a group of strangers.

If you are sending a group e-mail to colleagues in the office—memos, procedures involving the company, and other professional matters—a blind carbon copy is not necessary since you all work for the same company. If you have a departmental e-mail, it is also okay to send a memo that strictly pertains to the entire staff in that department. However, if one of those colleagues also needs to be addressed on something specific, do not include the matter in the group e-mail, as it wastes the group's time or, if it's of a sensitive nature, could embarrass the individual.

Group chain letters

Chain letters were bad enough when you were a kid, told that you would experience some fatalistic demise if you didn't respond within a certain amount of time. Group e-mail chain letters are generally unwelcome unless you know the members of your group well and are sure they want to receive such mail. If you receive such mail and don't have the time or tolerance for it, you should respond to the sender and politely ask him to please take you off his list.

E-tone

Keep aware that particularly with someone you don't interact with regularly, tone can easily be misinterpreted over e-mail. Without the receiver's ability to identify the inflection of your voice, facial expressions, or body language, messages have a greater chance of being questioned and overanalyzed. Misunderstood humor or sarcasm can easily lead to hurt feelings—another opportunity to revisit good old-fashioned common sense when communicating through electronics.

This is also how the emoticon was created. An emoticon is a symbol that shows the mood and tone. For example, a ;-) at the end of a sentence means the sentiment was meant in jest. Be careful not to overuse emoticons, as they can be annoying to the reader, like too many exclamation points in a written letter.

E-vites

When giving someone an invitation, calling and/or sending an invitation through the mail is always the preferred approach. If you send the initial invitation by e-mail, be sure to follow up with a phone call. Vital time can be lost if the message is not picked up and the occasion is close at hand.

E-thank-you notes

Is it appropriate to send a thank-you note electronically? Send an e-mail opposed to a handwritten letter only as a last resort. The old-fashioned phone call or card sent through the mail are still the preferred means of saying "thank you" after you've attended a dinner party or received a gift. Consider the effort your host went through in orchestrating such an event and her generosity to invite you. If it comes down to an e-mail, note, or nothing, opt for the e-mail. But remember, e-mail notes can become lost, overlooked, or not picked up right away. Also, electronic addresses change and computers systems falter. It might lead to an embarrassing situation if the person never received your thanks.

Sending bad news by e-mail

Don't send bad news by e-mail—it may not arrive. But beyond that, the receiver deserves to hear your voice. Being informed of the loss of a friend or relative by electronic means underscores the loneliness such a message can represent. Be sensitive to the effect of such words on the screen of a computer.

E-mail privacy

Whether you are sending messages at the office or from home, remember that there is no ironclad guarantee of privacy. Treat e-mail like an open note you might leave on a coworker's desk. Incidents of employees' losing their jobs because of offensive or controversial e-mail content, friendships that are lost over e-mail exchanges, and private information unnecessarily discovered are all precautions to be considered. There are stories of romantic affairs being discovered by the wrong person—let's just say that you want to avoid all such scenarios happening to you.

DO'S

1. Do be sure to reference the subject you are in an e-mail.
2. Do check to be sure that your business contact prefers e-mail to a fax or call.
3. Do use proper grammar and punctuation.
4. Do address the recipient by first or last name or a brief salutation.
5. Do try to acknowledge messages in a timely fashion.
6. Do designate all extremely personal dialogue to a phone call.
7. Do ask correspondents who bombard you with frivolous e-mails to take your name off their mass-mailing lists.
8. Do respect busy schedules by avoiding counterproductive questions.

DON'TS

① Don't continue to e-mail the person of an unreturned message.

② Don't gossip (especially about the boss).

③ Don't pass along off-color jokes or offensive language.

④ Don't abuse personal e-mailing.

⑤ Don't feel obliged to open "junk" e-mail.

⑥ Don't forward sensitive e-mail messages.

⑦ Don't use e-mail to discuss personal or interoffice complaints or problems.

Netiquette: Chat Rooms and the Internet

Sometimes conversations on the Internet are like being set up on a blind date at a potluck dinner. You have no idea what you're getting yourself into. For example, I was recently surfing the World Wide Web in search of a chat room discussing arthritis. I briefly settled in a room where people were sharing ways to manage back pain. A physical therapy student offered some tips and another person said he could cure back pain with some potion and offered his e-mail address. Then, suddenly, someone began talking about impotency and everyone got an earful of some very private confessions. I left that room and entered another advertising a discussion on the pros and cons of using Ritalin for Attention Deficit Disorder (ADD). Knowing some people whose children take Ritalin for ADD, I was interested. In seconds I realized I had crashed a private party. From one woman selling her jewelry to another discussing her grandmother's illness, the conversation slowly digressed into irrelevant chatter. As from a cocktail party gone haywire, I decided to make a subtle early exit.

Cyberspace can be a strange place because the standard ways of meeting and making introductions cannot exist. You do not shake hands. You do not look each other in the eye. You do not meet through friends. Typically you do not meet at all, let alone in the common physical way. Anonymously, you communicate. Anonymity can also foster laziness. You don't have to dress for the event and there is no uniform schedule or agenda to follow. So what are the rules?

In the early days of chat rooms and newsgroups, there were no rules. Newcomers logged on and observed. Sometimes what they saw was not very pleasant: people calling each other names, making unflattering assumptions, morphing from one persona to another, getting personal, monopolizing the conversation. Quickly discovering that such an environment is more prone to uncivilized behavior, ethics became increasingly important and Netiquette was born. The Computer Ethics Institute has formally addressed these issues in *The Ten Commandments for Computer Ethics,* as follows:

1. Thou shalt not use a computer to harm other people.
2. Thou shalt not interfere with other people's computer work.
3. Thou shalt not snoop around in other people's files.
4. Thou shalt not use a computer to steal.
5. Thou shalt not use a computer to bear false witness.
6. Thou shalt not use or copy software for which you have not paid.
7. Thou shalt not use other people's computer resources without authorization.
8. Thou shalt not appropriate other people's intellectual output.
9. Thou shalt think about the social consequences of the program you write.
10. Thou shalt use a computer in ways that show consideration and respect.

Cyberspeak

Certain conversational clues, and some inhibitions that are present when you meet in person or on the phone, are missing when you can't see or even hear the voice of your conversational partner. Occasionally an offensive remark made in cyberspace will be completely unintentional. People tend to speak more abruptly and are less cautious. The social graces honored when entering a social function should be followed when entering a chat room—despite the dramatically different atmospheres, many of the same rules apply.

Flaming is the act of attacking an individual on a personal level. Naturally, most everyone is opposed to such mean-spirited treatment. Do not comment on people's religions, relationships, personal habits, etc. If the conversation leads to such precarious subject matters, you should always support your comments with facts.

Spamming is another Internet term. It is the act of soliciting a service or trying to endorse a product, using advertising or a sales pitch, over e-mail or the Internet. No one wants to be spammed. Don't do it.

Plagiarism

If the Internet had been around during my school days, who knows if I would have ever seen the interior of a library. The access to any kind of information at a click of the mouse will keep musty books musty. The Internet also raises the question of plagiarism. As easy as it is to copy an appropriate paragraph from a textbook, it's even easier to do a cut and paste. Always openly and clearly credit the words and ideas of others. If using copyrighted material, the same rules apply to the computer screen as they do to the page. Be vigilant. Don't ever plagiarize. Finally, teachers have to be more aware of the endless options the Internet allows their students while students need to learn for themselves.

DO'S

1. Do try to spell correctly and use appropriate language, but don't point it out when others fall short.
2. Do think about how your statements and comments will be read by someone who doesn't have a history with you.
3. Do stick to the topic predetermined in a discussion group.
4. Do avoid private conversations in public forums.
5. Do use "emoticons" to indicate tone—tilt your head to see the emoticon smile:)

DON'TS

① Don't use chat rooms and other personal Internet activity on office time.

② Don't impersonate someone else or be dishonest about your profile.

③ Don't capitalize words, which is considered shouting. It's more pleasant to *keep your voice down*.

④ Don't use advertising or sales pitches (spamming) in unrelated discussions.

⑤ Don't "Spam."

⑥ Don't spread rumors.

⑦ Don't make any rude judgments about others (flaming) without having the facts to support your statement.

Telephones, Cell Phones, and Related Accessories

Cellular phones

You would never consider taking an alarm clock into the theater and risk it going off in the middle of a play. Yet, when it comes to the cell phone, we all seem to forget how disruptive the ringing can be (not to mention an entire conversation that follows).

Recently I went skiing with a friend who insisted on bringing her cell phone out on the slopes. She answered every call, which not only interrupted our time together, it also endangered us and other skiers. Finally, I knew I had to speak up. "This is getting a bit annoying," I said. "But more than that, it's dangerous to keep stopping for these calls. It might be better if you let the calls go while we're skiing. You can return them once we get to the lift." If I hadn't forced myself to speak up, I would have been resentful, and I'm too old to hold a grudge against a friend.

Common courtesy to others should trump our personal convenience. For example, if my assistant calls me with an urgent matter while

I am in a meeting, we keep the exchange very brief. Despite the obvious convenience, I would not dream of asking what other messages I might have. This goes to the heart of good manners. Before you go to a meeting or dinner party with your cell phone or beeper, ask yourself three questions: Do I have an urgent reason for taking it with me? Will it disturb others? Can I make an alternative arrangement for messages through voice mail?

Answering the phone during dinner was always forbidden at our home. This rule still applies now that the phone can be brought to a restaurant. If you find that you are often expecting urgent calls, use a vibrating beeper or one with a message readout and choose a cell phone that records messages. Give yourself as many options as you can to be accessible to those who need to reach you without being intrusive to those around you. And when your beeper notifies you of a call, excuse yourself from your company and find a private, quiet place to take the call.

The manufacturers of pay phone booths originally designed etiquette-friendly ones with doors. There are two reasons for the doors: They keep outside noise down and they provide a measure of privacy for the person making the call. Create artificial doors around yourself when you make or receive a call on a cell phone in a crowded place. In other words, don't share your private life with strangers—it's awkward and irritating for everyone.

The cell phone can also induce dangerous situations. Not only was my ski companion exemplifying poor manners by schussing and speaking; she also put herself and others at risk. Consider any activity that demands your attention an inappropriate venue for cell phones—driving, biking, or even crossing a street. On the first day of the new century, Suffolk County New York became the first county in the United States to make it illegal to use a handheld cell phone while driving a vehicle. Less than a week later, cell phones were deemed unwelcome in legislators' meetings.

If you do receive a call while you're behind the wheel of a car, it's best to either stop what you are doing so you can properly attend to the call or ask your passenger to take the call if possible.

Remember the following tips when using your cell phone:

DO'S

1 Do respect those around you when using your phone.

2 Do keep your voice down.

3 Do take calls in a private or separate area that is quiet whenever possible.

4 Do turn your cell phone off, or switch it to vibrate, at business meetings, restaurants, and public places.

5 Do keep conversations short and to the point if you are forced to take a call in the company of others.

6 Do make every effort to be accessible to *important* calls without disturbing those whom you are with.

DON'TS

① Don't put your cell phone down on the dining table.

② Don't try to walk around while on a call—you may move into a dead zone.

③ Don't talk to someone else (the waiter, someone on the street, etc.) while on the phone. It's disorienting and disconcerting for the caller.

④ Don't discuss private matters—such as relationships or finances—in public places.

⑤ Don't talk about other people by name in a public space.

⑥ Don't use inappropriate language.

⑦ Don't drive and dial; ask your passenger to assist in making the call or pull over.

Beepers

Beepers were originally devised for professional purposes: doctors who need to be on call at any given notice to attend to a patient or workers who do not adhere to regular business hours and are not always reachable at an office. Naturally, when duty calls (or beeps) these individuals may be interrupted at an inopportune time—at a dinner party, social gathering, or restaurant.

However, the beeper has found its way into the pockets and onto the belt loops of average citizens. Couples can send messages to each other when traveling, working mothers can communicate with their children throughout the school day. As with the mobile phone, such conveniences should not be abused, and the same etiquette should apply. Using a beeper for frivolous matters is not only discourteous but it also undermines the importance of a message made for more urgent purposes.

Phone-tiquette

For those who place a call and get an actual, live voice, it's only natural to find yourself out of practice on what to do. When telephoning, it's polite to ask: "Hello, this is Jason Hamilton. May I please speak with Serena?" The recipient of the call then says, "Just a moment please," if the call is not for them, or "Serena is not available. May I take a message?" If the caller does not identify himself, and the person being called cannot come to the phone, the person who answers the phone should say so *before* asking the identity of the caller. Otherwise it would appear that Serena is either avoiding the call or only answering to a select group. If you are screening your calls, let the person answering the phone know ahead of time to whom you do or do not wish to speak.

I have one friend who calls me and immediately begins by saying, "What are you doing?" As a general rule, you should never assume that the person you're calling will know who you are. It's polite to introduce your-self every time.

Business calls

It's expected that an office assistant answering the phone will ask who is calling, since he may be in a position to help. If the caller begins speaking without identifying herself, the assistant should speak up and ask, "May I ask who is calling please?" and the purpose of the call can be more effi-ciently handled.

In some businesses (notably doctors' offices) receptionists must attend to so many calls that they instantly put the caller on hold. Rather than answer the phone "Doctor's office," and then cut the caller off, inserting "please hold" or "just a moment please" is far more pleasant.

Personal calls

The luck of reaching a live voice has its considerations. Just because you reached your friend doesn't guarantee that he has the time to chat. Before entering a friendly conversation, it's always good manners to begin with "Is this a good time?" and then proceed to catch up. Likewise, a caller shouldn't call a friend only to cut it short by having to rush off to another appointment. Since it's difficult to keep relations alive and balance an active schedule, many people use the phone as a thoughtful reminder to check in as well as acknowledge their particularly busy agenda. If this is the purpose of the call, let it be known at the onset so the person you have reached is not offended by suddenly being cut short.

Off-hour calls

There are morning people and there are night people. For a morning person, there's nothing worse than hearing the phone ring at 11:30 P.M. By the same token, those who came home from a late evening out can't imagine anything worse than being awoken at 7:30 A.M. to a loud ringing sound. Always keep in mind whom you're calling before you do so at an off hour. A general rule is to call personal numbers from 9:00 A.M. to 10:00 P.M. during the week. On weekends, use your best judgment, as some people like to sleep in or, on the other hand, might keep later hours. This also applies to calling someone's cell phone.

Phone solicitors

When an unfamiliar voice calls for me, I always ask who it is. Once the speaker identifies himself as some form of cold caller or phone solicitor, I will then ask him to call back during office hours. If the caller is persistent and I have no interest in his sales pitch, I will cut to the chase and soon as possible and say, "Thank you, but I'm not interested," and hang up. If you feel like taking the time, you may also ask that, in future, the caller contact you by mail or, better yet, take your name off the call list, which usually gets the message across.

Call waiting

Call waiting is a tricky one. Let's begin with the name—Call *waiting*. Who likes to wait? I don't. Therefore I have never installed the device. However, there are polite ways to use call waiting. The first rule is to stay with the first call. You can put that conversation on hold and quickly take a message from a second caller, but you need to get right back to the original person. That is simple courtesy. If it is more urgent that you talk with the second caller, briefly explain the situation to the first person and ask if she would mind if you called her back. You might say: "I am sorry for the interruption, that is my daughter on the other line who is ill. May I call you back?" Or, "That is my husband and he has missed his plane."

If you know before you start the original conversation that an important call might come in, warn the person to whom you're speaking in advance. She will be much less irritated when you jump off if you have confided in her beforehand.

If you get several interruptions within the course of one conversation, the original person might become irritated. Or, conversely, if you are talking with someone who keeps jumping off the line to take another call, you might run out of patience. In this situation, it would be best to say: "Jane, may I call you another time when it is not five o'clock at night and everybody is trying to call us?"

Some phone companies allow you to disengage the call-waiting service for the duration of a very sensitive or important call by pressing ★70 or 1170 before making the call. Your phone book usually lists the services available, or contact your local phone service.

The abrupt sound of a busy signal can be equally as disconcerting for a caller as hearing a call-waiting tone. For those who do not have call waiting, try to keep calls short if you are expecting an important call, or consider an answering service or voice mail. Callers on the receiving end of a busy signal can contact their telephone provider—some companies offer a service that allows you to punch in a few numbers so your phone automatically rings back the party you are trying to reach once he finishes his call. Other options include the operator chiming in after their call is finished, forwarding him your message. Emergency breakthroughs, however, should be restricted to emergencies.

DO'S

❶ Do warn a caller that you may have to jump off the line if you are waiting for an important call.

❷ Do ignore incoming calls when you are on an important call. If the incoming caller persists, put the first party on hold and explain to the second caller that you will return her call.

❸ Do offer to get back to the initial caller if an ongoing conversation is interrupted more than once.

❹ Do treat the original caller as the primary line of communication.

❺ Do consider investing in a voice mail service that will forward incoming calls while your line is engaged.

DON'TS

① Don't use call waiting to get rid of a conversation.

② Don't put up with a friend who constantly jumps off the line for another call.

③ Don't leave a caller on hold for more than one minute.

④ Don't make an emergency breakthrough into a line unless the situation is urgent.

Answering machines

I have a niece who used to play almost an entire song on her answer machine, changing the song every week. Most of the time, I called her long distance and I didn't particularly want to listen to an entire song before leaving my message. It was so aggravating that I eventually left a message explaining that I would call less frequently if she didn't change her recording. Lo and behold, on my next call a few days later, there was a proper message: "Hello, I'm not home. Please leave your name and number and I will call you back at my earliest convenience."

Just as outgoing messages should be clear and succinct, incoming messages are best when brief and to the point. Do not leave a rambling message or one that is spoken so fast that the listener can't catch the name and phone number she needs to return the call. Leaving contact information at the beginning of a message and at the end of a message allows the person enough time to record the information. (So many times in frustration I've had to play a message over and over again to record a number from a long garbled message—I give up.) In addition, do not leave a serious or grave message on an answer machine such as the notice of a death in the family. Anyone in the family could hear the message first, notably the children. Such news is difficult to take from a machine. Always imagine how the recipient will react.

If you encounter a situation when your schedule forces you to leave such a message, gently introduce the news by saying, "I'm sorry to have to leave this message on the machine, but I'm at the airport and won't have another chance to reach you. I have some very sad news . . ."

If the message you are leaving is timely and important, consider following up with a second phone call. Sometimes people don't get the message because a family member erases it or the answering machine malfunctions.

DO'S

❶ Do keep outgoing and incoming messages brief and cordial.

❷ Do speak slowly and distinctly when leaving both outgoing and incoming messages.

❸ Do listen to messages and return calls as soon as you can.

❹ Do leave a number where you can be reached at the end of the message unless you are certain the recipient knows.

❺ Do convey urgent messages by saying: "I have important news. Please call me at your earliest convenience."

❻ Do leave your contact information twice so the recipient has time to record the information.

DON'TS

① Don't leave a grave or upsetting message on someone else's machine unless absolutely necessary.

② Don't leave a message that may be inappropriate for under-age ears.

③ Don't assume that your message was received.

④ Don't leave a long-distance number on an answering machine. Instead, tell the recipient you will call again at a stated time.

Voice mail

The creation of voice mail began a little game commonly known as telephone tag. Once again the evolution of telecommunications has left us with many situations where we inevitably don't connect. Take, for example, the person who leaves extended messages on voice mail due to the frustration of many thwarted attempts to get a live voice. While this process may be therapeutic for the caller, it can be a real inconvenience for the receiver who must listen to a lengthy message. If you are the caller, try to avoid this by saying: "This is my fourth attempt to reach you, please return my call so we can discuss a pending matter. I will be at 555-7692 between two and four P.M." Another consideration is to follow up with specifics via fax or e-mail.

Checking your machines when you are away

It is not necessary to leave an outgoing message on your machine that you will be away. In fact, for security reasons, I would not. Prior to your leaving, just make certain that those who depend on you know that you will be out of town. Otherwise you may either check your messages from remote and return calls as necessary or wait until you return to deal with callers, so as not to spoil a well-earned vacation!

Office voice mail

Contacting a company that directs all calls to a voice mail system is, at times, a laborious process. With many channels to go through, you may eventually be left with a disconnection. Prepare yourself by taking notes while listening to the recording or get direct extensions of the person you wish to contact. If you are installing a voice mail system for your company or home office, do your research. An onerous system could frustrate a client or jeopardize potential business opportunities. Leave professional messages on a company recording in addition to your office's personal line. For example: "This is Jane Rogers of Clyde Industries. I am not in the office right now, so please leave a message and I'll return your call as soon as possible."

Checking messages from outside the office or while away on trips is another benefit. Just be sure to leave an outgoing message that you will be out of the office and either direct the caller to the number where you can be reached, the receptionist, or an assistant. You should also consider leaving a recording that says you will be checking messages in a timely fashion.

Home office voice mail

Small businesses are the way of the twenty-first century now that setting up office can happen anywhere with just a laptop, phone, and letterhead. Naturally, these companies depend on the phone. Before setting up your home office, research the best phone services and take advantage of the options that suit your needs. Two lines should be strongly considered. Another option is to have the callers immediately connect to voice mail if you are on another call or connected to the Internet.

Speakerphones

Speakerphones are a great tool for professional matters, notably business affairs where many individuals need to connect to a party away from the office. They also allow mobility while on the phone (multitasking). Though the speakerphone's efficiency is the reason behind its existence, it can leave the caller on the other end of the line feeling that her call is interrupting more urgent matters. It may also inhibit her from relaying her intended message—it can be intimidating to speak to a room of people whose faces you cannot see. Such a forum also makes it easy for participants to speak out of line. At the beginning of the call, identify everyone who is privy to the conversation. Be careful not to cut anyone off, and allow each person to express his or her complete thoughts.

Answering a call through speakerphone rather than picking up the receiver demonstrates a genuine unwillingness to attend to the call. As ridiculous as they look, headphones can eliminate the self-important effect of a speakerphone.

Special phone services

Remember when mischievous callers could disconnect without acknowledging their identity? With the invention of call-back devices including *69 and caller ID—some of the best telecommunication services that promote good phone manners—prank calls are so "past century." Such services also come in handy if you are home but unable to get to the phone in time.

If you are able to be directed to the mystery party whose call you missed, you are then put in the position to properly identify yourself. In some instances you may recognize the person's voice, otherwise just identify yourself. For example, "Hello, this is Ms. Green and I am returning your call."

Most phone services make it possible for you to block your phone number from such caller ID services. Suffice it to say, however, abrupt hang-ups are not good etiquette.

I'm reachable?

Nowadays it is not only customary to have a home and office number but also a weekend number, cell phone, fax, and e-mail address. Such varied ways to be reached allows more possibility to be connected—so one would think. Who hasn't been a victim of return call overload? Or not being able to convey your message, thwarted by a brief yet unsuccessful communication via call waiting? With so many messages to return in a day, it is virtually impossible to get back to each call. No matter how daunting a task, and despite your busy schedules, every call from a friend or family should be returned. Caller ID and call forwarding are other devices to consider for the person who depends on receiving messages by phone.

What about unsolicited e-mails or phone messages from a company? It is only good behavior to return these calls as well. If time is a very real restraint, enlist your assistant or set a designated time to attend to these messages. Empathetically speaking, isn't it nice to have your messages returned?

Facsimiles

For me the fax machine is definitely a useful invention. I use it to send everything from documents and directions to plane schedules. For example, whenever I go to Detroit for a family-related board meeting, I fax one of my cousins to coordinate transportation to the meeting. The fax machine allows me to communicate with my Detroit and New York offices when I'm traveling, alleviating the inevitable pileup of paperwork I must face when I return. In fact, I recently took part in a real estate closing on property in Southampton, NY, from a boat in a very remote location off the coast of Spain. That transaction was possible thanks to the fax machine.

You should also keep in mind that the fax machine, in many instances, is in public view. If you fax or receive private messages and financial documents to and from an office, coworkers might be accidentally privy to such material. If the machine you are sending to is to a private home, be careful not to fax anything that is not appropriate for children. I am frequently asked if one can send an invitation by fax. Invitations should be sent by post. If, however, you have extra invites and are worried about them not arriving due to postal delays, it's more appropriate to make a phone call and follow up with a fax so the person you invite will have all relative details.

Faxes can also be fun. I love walking into the office to find a fax of my granddaughters' (ages five and eight) report cards sitting on my desk.

DO'S

 Do double-check all fax numbers before sending a document.

2 Do remember to remove the original document from the office fax machine.

3 Do call first if the machine you are sending to uses a shared phone/fax line.

4 Do follow up with a phone call if you fax an invitation.

5 Do type or write messages clearly. Faxes occasionally have poor readouts.

DON'TS

① Don't send an invitation by fax unless there isn't time to mail it.

② Don't fax a large document (over fifteen pages) unless the recipient approves.

③ Don't send anything to a family fax machine that is not appropriate for children to see.

④ Don't fax personal material to an office unless the recipient is waiting by the machine.

TAMING TECHNOLOGY QUIZ

If you receive a call on a cell phone at a restaurant you should:

A. Find out who is calling and ask to return the call at a more appropriate time.

B. Have a conversation if your dinner guest is late.

C. Excuse yourself from the table in order to take the call.

D. None of the above.

ANSWER: D; you should not have your cell phone on at a restaurant unless you are expecting an urgent call.

The proper way to address an e-mail is to:

A. Use the person's name in the salutation and sign off with yours.

B. Launch immediately into the message and sign off with your name.

C. Use the person's name in the salutation but not worry about signing off.

D. Any of the above.

ANSWER: A

You should return e-mails:

A. When your work schedule permits.

B. Within a day that you receive them.

C. On a weekly schedule that you've implemented.

D. None of the above.

ANSWER: B

If someone spells your name incorrectly in a chat room, you should:

A. Politely alert them to the error.

B. Not acknowledge the mistake and hope they will eventually notice.

C. Exit the chat room.

D. None of the above.

ANSWER: B

If you are trying to make a humorous point in a chat room, you should:

A. Spell words in capital letters.
B. Use emoticons.
C. Use italics.
D. None of the above.

ANSWER: B

In order of importance, when is it most appropriate to use a beeper?

A. Real estate agent trying to close a deal.
B. Children asking their parents if they can have a friend over.
C. A doctor attending to a patient.
D. Asking your spouse when he or she will be home for dinner.

ANSWER: C, A, B, D

If you are interrupted by call waiting with a more important call, you should:

A. Attend to the more urgent call and leave the original caller waiting.
B. Put that conversation on hold and quickly take a message from the second caller.
C. Explain the situation to the first person and ask if he would mind if you called him back.
D. Any of the above.

ANSWER: B or C

Which of the following is the best message for a home answering machine?

A. Hello, I'm not home right now. Please leave your name and number and I will call you back at the earliest convenience.
B. You've reached Anne Wilkes at 555-4286, please leave a message.
C. A catchy tune.
D. Any of the above.

ANSWER: A or B

In order of importance, when sending an invitation, it's best to:

A. Fax.

B. Phone.

C. Mail.

D. E-mail.

ANSWER: C, B, A, D

Expert Advice

Geraldine Laybourne, of Oxygen Media

Geraldine Laybourne is famous for her innovative television thinking, attitudes, and programming, via her role as the creative and business force behind building Nickleodeon and Nick at Nite throughout the 1980s and early '90s. Now, as Chairman and CEO for Oxygen Media, she is celebrated as an advocate for women, using her position and visibility to get their opinions heard.

As with any new technology, there's a learning curve, a trial of hits and misses, before understanding e-mail's proper function in our routine lives.

Admittedly I had a few mishaps when I first began using e-mail. Most notably was that my natural sarcasm, readily understood in person, was misinterpreted through e-mail. Those who know me can detect my sense of humor through the glint of my eye and tone in my voice. These gestures are naturally lost through e-mail. My attempts to parlay my particular sense of humor in writing—revealing my personality in an otherwise impersonal method of conversation—caused some hurt feelings.

An in-person discussion occurs quickly. We take for granted how our mannerisms guide the dialogue. Through e-mail a simple topic can be discussed numerous times before the actual point is ultimately made. People are also not as blunt in person as they can be over e-mail—where passive aggressive attacks are common. Over time, we will become more accustomed to this new method of communication, and it's worth it.

Just evaluate the outstanding benefits of e-mail as a business tool. It's no wonder that our economy prospers. The organization of an office without the paper bureaucracy of memos and business proposals—the efficiency is exhilarating. What may be most valuable is the democratization of an organization. From our West Coast studios to East Coast offices, our employees are able to communicate and work together despite the problems of distance and time difference.

E-mail has also helped revolutionize the foundation closest to my heart—family. Children are connected to grandparents who live far away, college students can ask their professors a question about their assignments, saving on phone bills, and correspondence can conform to everyone's busy schedule. What may be most rewarding is that taboo topics such as premarital sex, drugs, violence, and alcohol abuse are less intimidating through writing.

It's refreshing that the art of correspondence has come back in style with a turn-of-the-century twist. The routine thrill that one had when receiving the daily mail has now made a successful comeback through e-mail. I always appreciate the e-mails of one of my associates for his sincerity and his respect of gentility. His e-mails are absolutely distinctive. In time, everyone will find his or her own unique style. As I gradually discover my electronic voice, recipients of my e-mails will always know they're from me because of my digital signature—"Yup."

CHAPTER 11

EVERYDAY COURTESIES

*T*he most challenging moments of the day often seem to occur at the end of a workday, when we are tired and less prepared to rise to the occasion of politeness and civility.

Picture this typical scenario: You're about to board a plane and return from a long business trip. The attendant announces that the flight is overbooked and you are put on standby. If you were to sit back, accept the travel delay, and return to your book before awaiting further instructions, you deserve sufficient compensation in your next life for optimal behavior. If you're like the rest of us, chances are that attendant will soon become acquainted with your nasty side. While it's almost impossible to maintain civilized control under such circumstances, it is possible to handle the setback with manners. All that a complainer may get accomplished is a hoarse voice. Those who choose to work with the attendant may not only find that they will feel much calmer, they will probably see more results as well. At these most aggravating of life's little moments, shared by us all, it's the manner in which we choose to handle the challenge that separates the courteous from the discourteous.

Where's the Service in Customer Service?

We've all been through it. You attempt to call a doctor's office or a company's customer service department and are connected to so many incorrect lines or put on hold so interminably that when you finally get a human being on the line, you are ready to explode.

While it's only natural to get riled up, this approach usually accomplishes little. By taking a moment to collect yourself, you will probably be able to better rationalize the situation and properly assess your options. For the times when I encounter the rude salesperson, incompetent operator, or testy customer service representative, my strategy is to be overly friendly. Through this approach I can almost always snap another person's bad attitude into a helpful one. It's also sensible to ask the person politely for his name, not only because this may be helpful in your future contact, but then the representative loses his anonymous persona.

Communicating in Public Places

The world used to be a quieter place, and I am not even addressing the arrival of the cell phone. Once the train, elevator, or lobby of a hotel was considered a silent zone—dialogue between people was kept to a considerate volume. Before I pop enough Advil to develop an immune reaction, I'd rather see this rule revisited. Keep your voice down in any public place.

Smiling

If someone were to ask me to hand over my wallet, it would be a lot easier for me to give it up if he had a smile on his face. Not to sound like a cheesy 1970s bumper sticker, but, "Smile, it will make you feel better." You and everyone else around you, to be more precise.

While the latest trend in facial expressions seems to follow the hard-ened pseudo-sultry stares of pouty runway models, the sidewalk seems a sorry platform for iciness. As unpleasant a look as this is in public, I am es-pecially concerned by how many people choose to stare blankly during a job interview or when meeting someone for the first time. Such an im-pression is hardly a positive one.

I also have concrete research to support the healthy effects of smiling. In a study conducted by the University of California at San Francisco, women whose yearbook pictures showed bright smiles were more likely to be more mentally focused, have better marriages, and achieve an overall sense of joy throughout their lives.

I have a personal game with myself that involves getting all of those smile-challenged people around me to start grinning again. I try to return every sour expression with an excessively ebullient smile. And, happily, it usually works.

How to Treat People with Disabilities

Physically challenged people want to live independent lives with dignity. Your greatest assistance to someone who is disabled can be to treat him or her as a regular individual. If you suddenly feel awkward when in contact with a disabled person, remember that she is just like everyone else aside from the limitations of her disability. Eddie McPhee, the winner of CBS's first *Big Brother,* who lost a leg from cancer, says that you should read the signs from the individual. "For me it's an icebreaker to address it right away. I feel that it is easier for people around me to not have to try and fig-ure out how I lost my leg. You can move on, and then get to really know that person."

The National Easter Seal makes the following recommendations:

People with disabilities are entitled to the same courtesies you would extend to anyone, including personal privacy. If you find it inappropriate to ask people about their sex lives, or their complexions, or their incomes, extend the courtesy to people with disabilities.

If you don't make a habit of leaning or hanging on people, don't lean or hang on someone's wheelchair. Wheelchairs are an extension of personal space.

When you offer to assist someone with a vision impairment, allow the person to take your arm. This will help you to guide, rather than propel or lead, the person. Treat adults as adults. Call a person by his or her first name only when you extend this familiarity to everyone present. Don't patronize people who use wheelchairs by patting them on the head. Reserve this sign of affection for children.

IN CONVERSATION

- When talking with someone who has a disability, speak directly to him or her, rather than through a companion who may be along.
- Relax. Don't be embarrassed if you happen to use common expressions, such as "See you later" or "I've got to run," that seem to relate to the person's disability.
- To get the attention of a person who has a hearing disability, tap the person on the shoulder or wave your hand. Look directly at the person and speak clearly, slowly, and expressively to establish if the person can read your lips. Not everyone with hearing impairments can lip-read. Those who do will rely on facial expressions and other body language to help understand. Show consideration by facing a light source and keeping your hands and food away from your mouth when speaking. Shouting won't help, but written notes will.
- When talking with a person in a wheelchair for more than a few minutes, place yourself at the wheelchair user's eye level to spare both of you a stiff neck.
- When greeting a person with a severe loss of vision, always identify yourself and others who may be with you. Say, for example, "On my right is Andy Clark." When conversing in a group, remember to say the name of the person to whom you are speaking to give vocal cue. Speak in a normal tone

of voice, indicate when you move from one place to another, and let it be known when the conversation is at an end.

- Give whole, unhurried attention when you're talking to a person who has difficulty speaking. Keep your manner encouraging rather than correcting, and be patient rather than speak for the person. When necessary, ask questions that require short answers or a nod or shake of the head. Never pretend to understand if you are having difficulty doing so. Repeat what you understand. The person's reaction will guide you to understanding.

COMMON COURTESIES

- If you would like to help someone with a disability, ask if he or she needs it before you act, and listen to any instructions the person may want to give.
- When giving directions to a person in a wheelchair, consider distance, weather conditions, and physical obstacles such as stairs, curbs, and steep hills.
- When directing a person with a visual impairment, use specifics such as "left a hundred feet" or "right two yards."
- Be considerate of the extra time it might take a person with a disability to get things done or said. Let the person set the pace in walking and talking.
- When planning events involving persons with disabilities, consider their needs ahead of time. If an insurmountable barrier exists, let them know about it prior to the event.

(Courtesy National Easter Seals, www.easterseals.org)

Being Neighborly

It's both possible and acceptable to be a good neighbor without having to be your neighbor's best friend. In New York City, for example, apartment dwellers can go months without actually seeing the people who live in the apartment just six feet across the hall. In smaller towns, on the other hand, anonymity can be a bit harder to secure. In any situation, the most important thing is to treat neighbors with courtesy. Leaving unsightly garbage on your lawn or continually playing loud music is disruptive to those who share your residential area.

If you are having a party and anticipate loud noise, it's always polite to notify neighbors in advance, but don't feel you have to get their permission. Invite neighbors with whom you are on a friendly basis, but don't be offended if they decline.

How and When to Complain

I have a friend who couldn't understand why the tenant in the apartment above hers insisted on jumping rope at five in the morning. As the art of complaining is a ticklish one, my friend was nervous that her complaints would signify a declaration of war. However, after weeks of interrupted sleep, her energy and rest depended on it.

Finally, one morning she put on a bathrobe and went to confront her neighbor. It turned out that the woman was not jumping rope but rather packing suitcases in spiky stilettos. She operated a bicoastal company and needed to travel to L.A. a few times a week on the earliest flight. After the tenant saw my friend in her sorry state, she apologized, promised to pack at a more reasonable time, and assured her that she wouldn't wear her heels in the house.

If your neighbor is not as accommodating and a chronic offender, reread your lease to see what rights you have. Contact your landlord and, if possible, have other tenants cosign your letter.

An even more unsettling problem is how to handle the couple that continually fights. Interfering with other people's personal drama can be unsettling for everyone, and you can never predict how someone will act toward you when in an irrational state. If a fight sounds dangerous, call the police before it turns into something you may read about in the papers the next day.

Road Rules

It's not enough to drive safely. There will always be that impatient speeder, that person who steals your parking spot, and other drivers who test your poise. A moving vehicle is a dangerous machine. Never use your car to teach another driver a lesson. If someone abruptly cuts you off in the fast lane, it is critical to try to relax and avoid the impulse to get back at such an infuriating driver.

When a man drives a woman, she is not expected to wait in the front seat to be attended to like a hothouse flower. If the driver unlocks the car door on the passenger side to allow you in, it's always polite to reach over and unlock the driver's door.

Giving Up Your Seat on Public Transportation

On a crowded bus or train, one gives up his or her seat to someone who is elderly, pregnant, has a small child, or is weighted down with packages. Now that men and women lead independent lives, and the myth of the weaker sex has been shattered, men are no longer expected to jump up and offer their seat to the weak and tired lady.

Past Century/ Present Century

Back in the days of unpaved streets and horse-drawn carriages, when a man and a woman strolled together, the man always walked on the outside to protect a woman from splashing buggies. Once street conditions were made less primitive, the woman remained on the man's right. Now that walking is so casual and the idea of any formal rules could cause sidewalk gridlock, do what you please. A group of friends, however, should walk no more than two abreast, in order not to obstruct traffic.

However, if you find that you are depleted of any energy and the thought of standing makes you feel knobby at the knees, it's not mandatory to give up your seat to an elderly person.

Giving Advice

I have one friend who puts on the therapist hat with every issue, even when I don't have issues with the issue. While it's thoughtful to have concerns and look out for your fellow acquaintances, sometimes unsolicited advice is best kept to oneself.

Past Century/ Present Century

"Ladies first," doesn't always apply, notably when getting into taxis or the backseat of a car. A lady may want to enter after the man for a number of reasons—clothes, your back, etc. If the man holds the door open, I will say, "Do you mind getting in first?"

Accepting Compliments

For some, being faced with a compliment is like being told that your zipper is undone. Embarrassment takes over and suddenly the person overcompensates, protesting the compliment with a self-deprecating remark. Remember, this response may also embarrass the person giving the compliment. Always accept a nice word with grace and a thank-you.

With Friends Like These

She drops you as quick as a dot-com stock once a new guy enters the picture. You were promoted to partner and suddenly your Tuesday night basketball partner has other plans. When things are bad, there's no shortage of shoulders to lean on, but what about when things are good? People are capricious by nature and any friend will have those moments of irrational behavior. True friends, though, come through in good times and bad and are worth making the added effort for. Chances are they earned a role in your life based on a genuine sharing, trust, and loyalty.

If a friend has hurt you, it's your responsibility to tell her so, and you both owe it to the friendship to work things out. The option is far superior, and more polite, to holding a secret grudge.

The Friend Who Rarely Commits

He's canceled for the third time in a week, and hasn't returned your latest e-mail or phone messages. If you know someone like this and he's hurting your feelings, establish whether this friend deserves a place in your life, and, if so, confront him directly or write a note expressing your feelings and that you would like an explanation for this recent behavior. I recently confronted a friend who continually neglected my attempts to call her. Finally I left a message on her machine saying, "Stacey, please call me as soon as you can—I would really like to speak with you." Hours later she returned the call, apologizing for her especially busy workload. I then apologized for my neediness, but told her that simply returning my calls would put my regressive school yard insecurities at ease.

For the one doing the blowing off, keep in mind that a friend's feelings are attached. You should always make the effort to return someone's message with a genuine explanation, such as, "Sorry it's taken me a while to get back. I've been under deadline at work and am trying to get everything settled before I leave for London next week."

When a Friend Embarrasses You

There are some people who have a skill for keeping a discussion going at the expense of others. If you have a friend who finds it entertaining to bring up personal stories about you, making you feel uncomfortable, he may not be aware of your unease. You may say, "Can we save this story for another time?" If you want to make your message stronger, say, "Wait! That's embarrassing to me, you'll have to keep it to yourself."

If your companion makes loud comments about the people seated at the next table, you may say, "Can you please keep your voice down? I'm sure those people can probably hear you. I don't think we should be talking about them." For the incident where a friend tells an anecdote of questionable taste, possibly while riding in an elevator or on line at a movie, you may say, "Can we save this story for another time? When we're not in public?"

Introductions

Making an introduction may seem fairly standard. But when the occasion requires a slightly greater effort, it's good to be prepared with a more polished presentation.

Include both first and last names of those whom you are introducing, even if this is an introduction in a professional setting where there is a difference in balance of power. During introductions, all people are people. Don't invoke social hierarchy by calling the chairman "Ms. Thomas" and the less exalted assistant "Ralph." The only people I introduce by their first names are children.

You may want to include some relevant personal information so it makes it easier for those being introduced to mingle. For example, "This is Kevin Hartman, whose children go to the same school as the Rosens' kids." I have one friend who introduces people with such wit and irreverence, it puts everyone in a giddy mood. She'll say, "This is Jared Westerly, the next prince of New York." Or, "This is Casey Livingston, who just turned down the proposals of four media barons and has an eight-million-dollar deal to sell her memoirs."

Refrain, however, from turning the introduction into a sales pitch. You don't have to be responsible for your companions' networking nor should you have to trumpet the achievements of your friends. Keep Thoreau's words in mind: "I do not judge men by anything they can do. Their greatest deed is the impression they made on me."

Shaking Hands

The art of shaking hands appears to have some serious competition with the high five, locking thumbs, and other greetings that seem more appropriate for the baseball dugout. Unless one person knows the other and the two have a shared rapport on how to greet each other, it's best when meeting someone new to extend your hand in the traditional manner to avoid any confusion. As hip as one appears, not everyone is up on the latest handshake.

Social Kissing

Kissing on the cheek is always a warmer introduction than the standard handshake. There are many styles—the double cheek European kiss, the sappy on-the-forehead kiss, or the air-kissing-diva method.

Past Century/ Present Century

Traditionally, when a man and woman met, the man waited for the woman to offer her hand. Nowadays a man need no longer wait. If a woman doesn't extend her hand immediately, a man may offer his.

There are also the bold kissers who aim directly for the lips. To avoid the latter, turn your head so the offender will miss the target. When initiating a social kiss, I would stick to the basic on-the-cheek version so not to seem pretentious or misunderstood.

Improper Questions

Asking someone about her income, relationships, or how old she is is naturally impolite—yet people still seem to ask questions of a personal nature. As rules in manners become more lenient, this one has not slackened.

For those bold enough to impose an improper question, a *little wit* can gently put offenders in their place. When my six-year-old granddaughter asked a family friend why he had gotten so fat, she was instructed on why such presumptuous behavior is impolite. When an acquaintance asked me who my therapist was, I told her: "I don't have one, but who is yours?"

Evading Personal Questions

To potentially embarrassing questions asked out of ignorance, I suggest a partial answer. For instance, a friend who had just seen her lawyer about a separation agreement was confronted at a cocktail party by a well-meaning acquaintance who asked about how her husband was. She replied, "He's been extremely busy at work." Her answer satisfied the questioner without giving away any personal particulars. If a question offends you, such as "How much did your CD player cost?," there's no need to be indignant. An evasive but polite answer is the best reply, such as "I don't remember" or "It was a gift."

When people ask tactless or antagonistic questions meant to put you on the defensive, you can do what certain politicians do so well—evade the question entirely. For example, "How come you aren't married yet?"—a question often put to single people by a smug newlywed—may be countered with, "Are you about to propose?" Or, less coyly, "I'm flattered by your interest in my personal affairs but I'm baffled as to why you're so curious."

Taking Your Foot Out of Your Mouth

Let me pose a few scenarios:

1. You meet up with an old acquaintance who is expecting her first child. You say, "Congratulations, I heard about the wonderful news. When are you due?" She responds, "I had a little boy last month."

2. At a friend's lunch, you meet another woman who also has five children. You initiate the conversation by saying, "I don't know how I could have ever raised my kids properly in the city." She responds, "I raised my children in the city."

3. You are seated next to a colleague at a restaurant who is engaged. He is intimately nestled with another woman. You say, "Hello, Rick—it's nice to finally meet your fiancée." He responds, "No, this is my friend Leslie."

While each scenario is highly embarrassing, they happen. (And, yes, each of these situations are based on actual events.) The first lesson to be learned is that you should never assume anything in casual conversation. However, since the human species is known to err on occasion, you can handle an etiquette disaster with grace. This is one of those times when I advocate a little harmless fibbing. In scenario 1, for instance, you can handle the gaffe by saying, "I'm sorry, what I meant to say was that I heard you were expecting, I wasn't sure whether you had a boy or girl." Scenario 2: "You are so fortunate to have exposed your children to a cosmopolitan upbringing. My husband and I decided to move to the suburbs because it was more affordable." Whether or not your effort is believed, you did make a sincere attempt. As for scenario 3, since, again, you should assume nothing—a quick glossing over of your blunder is always best. Besides, it's not your indiscretion to truly worry about.

Chance Encounters

When you encounter a friend while you are out with another friend, it's polite to stop and chat for a moment, and introduce the person you are with. Then you can begin a casual discussion.

Unexpected meetings can be awkward if you are with that "special friend"—someone you are not prepared to let others know about quite yet. Leaving him by your side is doubly incriminating and will make the situation even more obvious. Don't feel obligated to explain who this person is—however, an introduction is standard.

Another embarrassing situation can occur if you forget someone's name, something I've been known do on occasion, especially when the face is out of context with its usual place. It's better not to bluff your way through the conversation. Instead you can confess and say, "I'm sorry, I've forgotten where we've met?"

By the same token, if you say hello to someone who stares at you blankly, help that person by introducing yourself, reminding him where you've met. It's not fair to expect people to play guessing games by saying, "Don't you remember me?" since you may receive a rude "No."

The Name Game

Ms. or Mrs.? Catherine or Cathy? There are many ways to address someone, but usually there's only one way a person likes to be addressed. This is learned through an introduction. If a person is introduced as "Matthew," unless they express otherwise—he should be referred to as such. It's always polite to ask, "Do you go by Matthew or Matt?" If someone continually botches your name, rather than privately be annoyed, direct her accordingly.

The Newlywed Woman

The modern newlywed has a choice to make when it comes to taking her spouse's name. Today's professional woman has often developed her career and contacts based on her birth name. For many, changing that name may disrupt her working life. Some women choose to maintain their maiden name with their career contacts while changing their names on legal documents. Others hyphenate the two names while some opt to not change their names. Rather than assume a woman has taken a new name, it's always proper to ask first.

How to Address Strangers

In social situations, introduce yourself by stating your entire name. If you are in need of assistance from a salesperson, "Excuse me, miss" to a young woman, or "ma'am" to an older woman is always polite. Sir is still standard when addressing a man. (For more on introductions, see Chapter V.)

DO'S

1 Do keep a calm demeanor when an unexpected mishap sets you back.

2 Do keep your voice down when speaking to others in public places.

3 Do accept a compliment with grace and a thank-you.

> ## Past Century/ Present Century
>
> *Way back when, children never spoke to adults on a first-name basis. While young children should still refer to adults by Mr., Mrs., or Ms., once they reach adulthood, it's permissible to be on a first-name basis. The older adult can initiate this with a simple, "Please call us Will and Darcy." However, I still call some of my mother's friends by their conventional titles, whether out of habit or tradition.*

4 Do answer an improper question with a little wit.

5 Do gently correct someone if he calls you by the wrong name.

6 Do introduce yourself to strangers using your whole name.

7 Do speak directly to someone who has a disability.

8 Do warn neighbors beforehand if you are having a party.

DON'TS

① Don't avoid issues with a friend that are upsetting you; discuss them.

② Don't be in the habit of giving unsolicited advice to friends.

③ Don't make personal assumptions of an acquaintance based on casual conversation.

④ Don't shorten or change someone's name from the one she used when introduced.

⑤ Don't assume that a woman has taken her husband's name.

⑥ Don't lean on someone's wheelchair.

⑦ Don't ignore someone's message just because you are especially busy.

EVERYDAY COURTESIES QUIZ

Once connected to the right customer service representative after being rudely misdirected, you should:
    A. Ask him his name for future reference.
    B. Complain and use another service.
    C. End the call since such a company is unable to perform a simple task.
    D. Find out who the superior is so you can file a complaint.
ANSWER: A

If a couple in your building is having a fight that sounds as if it could be dangerous:
    A. Slip spousal abuse literature underneath their door.
    B. Knock on the door and ask them to quiet down.
    C. Speak with other neighbors and try to have them evicted.
    D. Call the police.
ANSWER: D

When a friend is telling a rude story in a public place:
    A. Ask her to save the story for later in a more appropriate environment.
    B. Pretend that she is not with you.
    C. Apologize to those around you for your friend's improper behavior.
    D. Act like nothing is wrong.
ANSWER: A

When introducing people to one another:
    A. State only their first names.
    B. State only their last names.
    C. Include both first and last names of the people you are introducing.
    D. Any of the above.
ANSWER: C

CHAPTER III

TABLE MANNERS

*I*f you've ever had the displeasure of eating with a companion who uses his utensils like drumsticks or is under the impression he can articulate a sentence while chewing food, then you've surely realized that basic table manners are a necessity. However, some consider the rules of the table to be as daunting as learning Portuguese. The truth is, table manners are not difficult—they just take some practice. The best place to learn is at home. The most important thing is to eat naturally (being overly self-conscious will spoil your dinner). Eventually table manners will become second nature, a great reason to dine out and show off your new skills.

Not at the Table

"Being Set at meat Scratch not neither Spit Cough or blow your Nose except there's a Necessity for it."

George Washington,
Rules of Civility and Decent Behavior

I always refer to our nation's first president for some good tips in basic manners. While George Washington is commenting on the impoliteness of blowing one's nose at the table, this rule also applies to brushing your hair, filing your nails, or any other excessive primping. For women, a quick check in your compact, or application of lipstick, is acceptable. For an imminent nasal attack, make it quick and quiet. When you sneeze, use your tissue, or at least place your hand in front of your nose and mouth. Aside from times of dire emergency, a napkin is not a tissue.

Napkins on Your Lap

"Put your napkin on your lap." If there's one rule we've all had drummed into our heads a million times, this is it. So now that we know where we put it—when do we put it there, what do we use it for, and how long does it stay there? This piece of cloth has many rules attached to it. First, wait until the host begins to unfold her napkin before you do so; this signals the beginning of the meal. During business meals, it's customary to wait to put your napkin on your lap, as business may be discussed first. Always use your napkin to wipe your mouth before drinking so that you won't leave food on the rim of the glass.

Your napkin remains on your lap until after the meal. If you have to get up from the table during the table, leave your napkin on your chair so it doesn't get in the way of your dinner partner. When your host puts her napkin on the table, that is the signal for the end of the meal. Place the napkin loosely on the table (it should only be folded if you are placing it in a napkin ring).

The Formal Table Setting

A seated dinner where guests are served is considered a formal dinner. Place plates are at each setting when guests arrive at the table. The plate containing the first course, soup or fish, for example, is set directly on the place plate. Place plates are removed along with the plate from the first course.

The formal table is never set with more than three knives and three forks. Additional silver, a salad fork, for instance, is placed beside the plate when the course is served. The spoons for an appetizer such as fruit or soup are placed to the right of the knives. The dessert spoon and fork are placed above the plate. No serving dishes are ever put on the table, except dishes of fruit or candy. Condiments are served and returned to the kitchen. (see formal table setting below).

There's More Than One Fork?

A formal meal can be more daunting than delicious with all of that silver and glassware to handle. The simple rule to follow is to begin with silverware on the outside of the place setting and then work inward with each course. When in doubt, follow the host.

Unsanitary Service

A visit to the kitchen of some restaurants may make you decide to never eat out again. Knowing that the sanitary guarantee of your food and tableware is entrusted to those who serve you is reason why I am known to be extremely loyal to selected establishments. When dining out, at either a restaurant or private home, it's permissible to ask your waiter or host for a clean utensil or glass. For the "Waiter, there's something in my soup" scenario, it's entirely up to you if you'd like a fresh bowl.

Past Century/ Present Century

Finger bowls are a handy accessory, particularly for a meal of shellfish or corn on the cob. However, I stopped using them when recently a guest picked up his finger bowl and drank from it. Just one less thing for me to clear, I suppose.

Serving

At an informal meal, when the host serves, he or she passes each plate to the right. The person at the halfway mark keeps the first dish; others on the right keep each dish thereafter. The host then serves to the left, serving himself or herself last. Vegetables, sauces, and salad may be passed separately among the guests. When a waiter is serving, he presents each platter to the guest's left since it is easier for right-handed diners to serve themselves from this position.

Holding Utensils

There are those who can eat their way through a tough filet with the grace and ease of a violinist. My friend Allegra, who learned her table manners from her Italian grandmother, never really enjoyed the evening meal where the instruction took place. Her grandmother was so vigilant; Allegra had to keep books beneath her arms to keep her elbows from flapping around like a crazed chicken. For most of us, it's enough to just imagine that the books are beneath our arms.

There are two styles of eating—European or American. To eat in the European style, hold the fork in your left hand, tines facing down, the knife in the right, and then cut your entree. Still in your left hand, lift the fork, tines down, and bring to your mouth. The American method is to cut a bite, place the knife on the side of the plate, then switch the fork to your mouth.

For the left-handed minority, you should eat in a way that is most comfortable for you.

Dropping Silverware

We all do it. Suddenly holding your fork is like trying to hold a water balloon. If you do drop a piece of silverware, alert the nearest available waiter and ask for a replacement. If the waiter is not too busy, he can retrieve the fallen utensil and take it away. Otherwise, it is fine for him to pick up the piece after everyone has left the table. At a dinner party, you may pick up the utensil, wipe it off with a napkin, and return it to the table.

Holding Drinking Glasses

Holding a glass properly is for more than just wine snobs impressing one another with their knowledge of enological etiquette. How you hold your wineglass affects taste and temperature of your drink. Hold a red wineglass at the base of the bowl. Hold a glass of chilled white wine by the stem to keep it cool. Brandy snifters when first served are held at the base of the bowl with both hands in order to warm the brandy. Cup the snifter in one hand when you sip the brandy.

Toasts

"Nostrovia!" . . . "Sante!" . . . "Cheers!"—when it comes to toasting, we're all multilingual. Toasting is a custom that's commonplace in Europe. For our purposes, it shows that you can share good cheer even before you start drinking. Just keep it short and always avoid any blurts about past relationships when toasting a new couple. The tradition is to provide happiness, not harbor any ill will.

When entertaining, Margrit Mondavi, of Mondavi Wines, always begins her meals with a toast. "It may vary on the occasion," she says, "but I always keep it spontaneous." Her husband, Robert, adds, "Our table happens to be oval. I often offer people to toast the person next to them. It gets everyone in the mood. All you have to do is touch the glass and look at them in the eye, until it comes back to the host. This brings everyone together. You feel it from the heart—you want to welcome everybody. It opens you up and makes you want to exchange ideas."

Accidents at the Table

Don't cry over spilled milk. Or, in regards to table manners, don't make such a fuss when you have an accident at the table. Discreetly attend to a spill with your table napkin. A bit of food on the table can be scraped with the edge of a clean knife or spoon. A spill that could potentially cause damage or stain a tablecloth should be called to the host's attention.

Tongue and Teeth

So, you're out on a first date and you ordered the spaghetti with pesto sauce. I must say, it's a gutsy move to order a dish with such a high degree of edible difficulty on a first date, but if you love pesto sauce, that's your call. But now you're gripped by the fear that a piece of basil is caught between your front teeth. Whether it's paranoia or a legitimate sensory reaction, you must attend to this little green matter before it spoils your evening. Never use a toothpick at the table, which is akin to using a fork to clean your nails. Toothpicks are a strictly private matter. Take a sip, not a swig, from your water glass. If you feel this has not dislodged the pesky perpetrator, cover your mouth with your napkin and attend to the manner. Discretion is key, as it would be in poor taste to be overtly witnessed in this manner.

If you are on the receiving end of this toothy mishap, a gentle "You have something caught in your teeth" is admissible. Just remember that it's natural for your companion to become embarrassed, so keep the remark lighthearted. You may want to avoid the issue altogether. However, while this approach saves you from an awkward moment, your companion will only have to encounter this obvious mishap eventually. The other advice, just order the lemon chicken on important dinner dates.

Food for Thought

Following are some tips for eating foods that present the most confounding degree of difficulty:

Artichokes: Always eat artichokes with your fingers, one leaf at a time. Dip the pulpy leaf into the sauce and scrape off the meat with your teeth. Place the spent leaf on the side of your plate or in a separate dish provided. When you reach the prickly part (the choke), scrape it away with a knife and then eat the heart with a knife and fork.

Asparagus: Also finger food, notably when the stalk is small and slender. For thicker pieces it's easier to use your utensils, otherwise excess water and oil could be messy. Cut and eat one bite at a time, leaving the tough, inedible part on your plate.

Avocado: Cut avocado is eaten with a fork. Use a spoon to eat a halved avocado that is still in the shell.

Bacon: Truth again that finger food has its place at the formal dinner table. The crispness of bacon defies any attempt to use a knife and fork.

Bread and Butter: This one dates back to the Round Table. In medieval times, when bread was broken at the table, each piece was eaten separately so that leavings could be given to the poor. For your consumption purposes, begin by breaking off a bite-size piece of bread, and butter the piece while holding it against the side of the butter plate. Hot rolls, muffins, or toast should be buttered at once while the bread is still hot—luckily taste isn't sacrificed for custom on this one. To serve yourself from a butter dish, use the butter knife. If there is no butter knife, use your own if it is clean enough to service all of your buttering needs. If you need more butter, and your knife is dirty, ask your host for a new one.

Cheese: When served as an hors d'oeuvre, cheese is spread on crackers with a knife. When cheeses and fresh fruits are served for dessert, the cheese is cut and eaten with a fork. Runny cheeses such as Camembert and Brie are always spread on crackers with a knife.

Corn on the cob: Finger food, yes, but be sure to use both hands. A large ear may be broken in half to simplify.

Fish: When a small fish is served whole, begin by cutting off the head and tail; then slit the fish from one end to the other lengthwise and lift the meat (fillet) away and up from the backbone. Place the bones on the side of your plate or butter dish. Eat the fish with a fish fork or both the knife and fork. Be careful to take small bites and chew cautiously. If you find a bone in your mouth, take it out with your thumb and forefinger.

Fruits

Apples and pears: When eaten at the table, they should be quartered and then cored with a knife. You may then eat the quarters with your fingers or cut them into smaller pieces and eat them with a fork.

Bananas: Peel, then break and eat each bite with your fingers.

Grapefruit: When served in halves, as tempting as it may be, don't squirt excess juice onto your spoon. If served as a whole in a fruit bowl, you may peel it as you would an orange.

Grapes: Break or cut a section from a large bunch rather than pick individually. When eating a grape with seeds, put the whole grape in your mouth, drop the seeds into your fist, and then put them onto your plate.

Kiwis: Begin by peeling and cut in half. Then eat with a fork.

Mangoes: Cut into quarters; pull skin from each section while holding the slippery section down with a fork, then cut into bite-size pieces with a spoon or fork.

Melon: When a quartered melon is cut into sections from the rind, eat it with a fork. When it is not, cut the fruit away from the rind and eat with a spoon. Melon balls are eaten with a spoon.

Oranges: Section the skin with a knife and peel off. Break the orange apart and eat one section at a time.

Papayas: Served cut in half and should be eaten with a spoon.

Pineapple: Served in chunks and eaten with a fork.

Watermelon: Generally served on the rind and is usually eaten with both hands. Drop the seeds into your hand and then onto your plate. You can also eat with a knife and fork; begin by removing seeds with a fork.

Other Foods

Game birds, poultry: Use your knife and fork to remove as much meat as you can. Whole pieces of chicken are picked up only at picnics or other informal meals.

Pasta: Spaghetti is kiddy food, fun in that it is twirled around your fork and then lifted to your mouth. If the dish is served with a spoon, hold the spoon in your left hand and twirl the spaghetti into a nest in the spoon. Leave the spoon resting on the plate and bring the spaghetti to your mouth with the fork.

Pasta may be eaten with a fork; however, you can use a knife for bigger pieces like rigatoni and fusili.

Past, Past Century/ Present Century

Salad has evolved from a strictly fork food to a knife and fork meal. This is not so much due to the fact that today's hearty salads require the added effort of a knife, but because in the days before knives were made of stainless steel, the vinegar in the salad discolored the blades.

Pizza: Unless the pizza is runny, use your hands. It always seems to taste better to me without the knife and fork.

Salad: It's the misleading easy order for when you're trying to make a good dining impression. Alas, you inevitably come across a piece of lettuce as big as a banana leaf—panic ensues, and starvation seems a viable alternative. Rather than folding the lettuce with a fork, cut the lettuce with a knife.

Shellfish

Fried clams: Eaten with either a fork or your fingers.

Hard-shelled crabs: Pull off the legs with your fingers and suck out the meat—refrain from slurping like a straw. Then turn the body on its back on the plate and pick out the meat with an oyster fork. Crack the claws with a nutcracker.

Lobster: Such a delicacy is a hard nut to crack, which is why nutcrackers can assist. To begin, twist off the front claws, crack them with the nutcracker, and remove the meat with an oyster fork or nut pick. Next, break the tail off the body. The meat in the tail can generally be lifted out with a fork more easily than the meat in the rest of the lobster. You can then cut the meat with a knife and fork or, more informally, since you're probably up to your elbows in butter and lobster, you can pick up the tail and bite off a mouthful at a time. Then break off the leg and quietly suck out the meat. If you're up to it, the green tomalley and red roe of the lobster are edible.

Mussels: When served in a sauce, take the mussel out of the shell with a fork. You may pick up the shell and quietly sip out the remaining juice. The leftover broth is eaten with a spoon, or you may dunk a bite-size piece of bread into the dish. Discard empty shells on your butter plate or in a plate specifically provided for them.

Raw oysters and clams: To eat when served on the half-shell, hold the shell steady in one hand and lift the oyster or clam with the fork held in the other. Dip the shellfish into sauce and pop it into your mouth. You may pick up the empty shell and tip the remaining juice into your mouth. When eating steamed clams, remove the clam by the neck with your fingers. Holding it by the neck, dip it into the clam broth, and then into the melted butter. Eat the whole clam in one bite. Put the clam shells in the available side plate.

Shrimp cocktail: Eaten with an oyster fork. Large shrimp are speared with a fork and eaten a mouthful at a time. Leave the tails on your plate or in a cocktail napkin. If you don't have either, find the nearest receptacle.

Snails: Grasp each snail with the special tongs that are always served with the dish and pull the snails from the shell with a snail fork.

Soup: Served in either a cup or a bowl, soup is eaten with a soup spoon. The spoon should be moved away from you and then brought to your mouth. A jingle taught to small children, which always helps me is: "All the ships go out to sea, bringing food for you and me."

It is permissible to drink the remainder from a cup when cool enough. A shallow plate can be lifted lightly to avoid any disruptive noise.

Sushi: Give your knife and fork a night off; chopsticks are the chosen utensils when eating sushi. Use your chopsticks the way you would a pair of prongs—the only difference being that they are not attached. One stick is held in a stationary position and the other is moved. If you have rolled sushi, place the whole piece in your mouth if you can—these pieces fall apart easily when consumed bite by bite. If you are sharing pieces, never use your chopsticks as a serving utensil; this is considered bad manners in Japan. If serving chopsticks aren't available, sharing food should be served with the clean, top ends of your chopsticks. For large pieces of food, you may separate the food into small pieces with your chopsticks, or you just bite a piece off and put the rest back onto your plate.

Past Century/ Present Century

Recently I had my priest over for lunch. I assumed that we would begin the meal by saying grace. When he began to eat, I said, "Father, no grace?" He looked at me incredulously and said, "Grace?" Coming from the highest authority, it's safe to assume that grace is no longer the standard custom it once was.

DO'S

❶ Do ask the waiter for a clean piece of silverware if yours is dirty.

❷ Do begin at the outside and work your way in with each course when the table is set with multiple pieces of silverware.

❸ Do pass sauces, salads, and additional items on a table setting among other guests.

❹ Do politely alert your dining companion if he has something stuck in his teeth.

❺ Do break off pieces of bread and eat each piece separately.

❻ Do drink soup from a cup when it is cool enough.

DON'TS

① Don't use your napkin as a replacement for a handkerchief at the dinner table.

② Don't hold a glass of red wine by the stem of the glass.

③ Don't save toasts just for special occasions.

④ Don't make a big deal if you spill something at the table.

⑤ Don't make slurping noises when sucking the meat from a crab claw.

⑥ Don't serve a piece of sushi with your own chopsticks.

TABLE MANNERS QUIZ

A napkin should be left on your lap:
    A. Only when you are eating.
    B. For as long as your host has a napkin on her lap.
    C. Just for the main course.
    D. For the entire meal.
ANSWER: D

At a formal dinner, the salad fork should be placed:
    A. Next to the soup spoon.
    B. To the left of the butter knife.
    C. To the right of the butter knife.
    D. Beside the plate when the course is served.
ANSWER: D

If you drop your utensil at a restaurant:
    A. Go to the kitchen and replace it yourself.
    B. Ask the waiter to replace it.
    C. Apologize to everyone at the table and ask if someone has an extra.
    D. Pick it up discreetly.
ANSWER: B

At an informal gathering, the host serves dishes to his:
    A. Left.
    B. Right.
    C. There is no set rule.
    D. The host does not begin serving the meal.
ANSWER: B

Hold a glass of white wine by:
- A. The base of the bowl.
- B. The stem.
- C. Whatever is comfortable for you.
- D. None of the above.

ANSWER: B

Asparagus should be eaten with:
- A. Your fingers.
- B. Whatever way is comfortable for you.
- C. A knife and fork.
- D. All of the above.

ANSWER: D

Snails are eaten with:
- A. Your fingers.
- B. A knife and fork.
- C. A special tong.
- D. Any of the above.

ANSWER: C

Expert Advice

Robert and Margrit Mondavi, Mondavi Wines

A Great Place

Robert G. Mondavi remains the global emissary of American food and wine. His vision was to create wines in California that belong in the company of the great wines of the world. Having successfully achieved this goal, his wisdom as founder and Chairman Emeritus of Robert Mondavi now guides his sons and daughter in their leadership roles in taking the Robert Mondavi family of wines into the new millennium.

Robert and his wife of more than twenty years, Margrit Biever Mondavi, Vice President of Cultural Affairs at Robert Mondavi Winery, reside in Napa Valley. A pioneering woman of the modern-day California wine industry, Margrit Mondavi joined the winery in 1967, pursuing a life-long interest in uniting wine with fine arts, music, and culinary artistry. Under her direction, the Robert Mondavi Winery developed original cultural and culinary arts programs that are now benchmarks for the wine world. The Mondavis are noted patrons of the arts in the Bay Area and enjoy traveling to wine-growing regions and to exotic places.

A memorable place setting isn't about displaying the crispest, whitest linen or silver so polished that you can use it to see if you have a lipstick stain on your cheek. Anyone can replicate the tabletop from Tiffany's, but the host who can mirror his style onto the table will enhance any guest's experience.

The table settings created by Margrit Mondavi are so unique, you can recognize her flair the way you can match a brush stroke to a noted painter.

"Margrit is so creative with her setting," chirps Robert on his wife's skill. "She sets a table with extraordinary flowers or even branches and rocks that she finds from her walks—a creative feeling that is something new and different. Each setting is dictated by the season, but she always has personalized touches like handmade paper cards." Adds Margrit, "I create a drawing pertaining to the occasion, which adds warmth to the festivities. Since we entertain quite frequently, these are the spontaneous things we do that make it more whimsical, unique. Being an artist is helpful, but ribbons and nice touches are all it takes. I also decorate the table with a motif that works with the meal that we are serving. I have used fish, pigs, frogs, rabbits, and elements from nature—this is what distinguishes the table. It has become second nature. It's also infectious—the whimsy mood is to try and make our guests feel good."

But for all of the serendipity that distinguishes the Mondavis' table, there is some planning. Says Margrit, "First I look at the occasion—it may be an anniversary or friends visiting from out of town. I then look over the menu and then I start to think about the table decor. Other elements are woven in to the atmosphere, blending and creating a visceral experience. Happy music, the right lighting, and great wine are added touches that will be brought to a Mondavi table."

As for rules of etiquette, the Mondavis do take their wine seriously. "We are wine people," reminds Margrit. "You put out the wine, you will drink first from your glasses set at the right and then move inward. It's a sort of high etiquette that even has a certain style of glass. A Bordeaux will have a bigger cylinder and the dessert wine is served in a small glass. I don't like colored or etched glass for wine since wine is so beautiful on its own. The color, the texture—why conceal it?"

Both Mondavis work together in creating the menu. "We get wines that are unique, that blend together well with what we are serving, adding to the overall atmosphere." And, naturally, spirits add to the overall spirit.

The one task that Margrit Mondavi finds the most tricky is the seating arrangement. "I can scrub the floor and do the dishes, but to arrange the seating is the most difficult thing. If I have to do it myself, it's Russian roulette. Certain people feel that because of rank and position, they are entitled to be near Robert. I try to the best of my ability to seat people. If that doesn't work, sometimes I let the guests choose their own seats."

CHAPTER IV

DINING RIGHT

*T*he key to dining out is that it tastes great without the extra effort. Not only is the food prepared by an expert, but the greatest effort you must make is deciding on what to order. There's also no mess to clean and you can invite friends without having to worry whether you have enough seating. These days dining out is also a way to entertain. Tim and Nina Zagat, of the series of Zagat guides, point out that twenty years ago, it was routine to have people over to your home when you wanted to entertain, but now it is increasingly common to entertain at a restaurant. Not only are there benefits in not having to do any of the work, but it can also be more cost effective.

Whether it's for a quick slice of pizza or a three-course meal at the latest hot spot, dining in a restaurant allows you to experience a whole new atmosphere and to pick up on the buzz and energy of those around you. Listening in and observing the behavior of others can most certainly be more intriguing than whatever's on television that night—not that I make it a routine to listen in to other people's conversations. So now that you can practice your polished table manners in public, here are a few other rules of etiquette that apply exclusively to dining out.

Reciprocating Plans

In today's chaotic world, trying to make a dinner plan with a friend can sometimes seem as difficult as arranging a summit meeting between world powers. Arrangements may often be negotiated between assistants, there are always a few last-minute cancellations, and, inevitably, you must compromise your schedule to some degree in order to meet your friend's. Before a never-to-be-met dinner plan causes a temporary rift, keep in mind that we're all busy.

Confirmations should be made before noon of the day of the plan so that the party canceled on can rearrange his or her evening.

The Customers' Rights

The restaurant business is a service business. In a sense, the restaurant's owner and staff are working for you to ensure a pleasant experience. It's basically their job. As Tim Zagat outlines:

1.   The customer is always right.
2.   Short of a patron throwing bombs, if a customer is wrong, read rule one.

Reservations

When making a reservation, always begin by being pleasant on the phone. On the day of your reservation, don't forget to confirm. An organized restaurant typically calls you the day you are expected, sometimes even a few days before. If you are going to be late or if you need to add or subtract a guest from the table, these are also essential details the restaurant needs to know. "We prepare food in advance for a certain number of people. Even if it's the last minute, we can give a table to someone who just walked in," says Amy Sacco, owner of Lot 61 in New York City. Tim Zagat also understands the importance in canceling. "It's vital to the restaurant and the customers; if you don't cancel, it hurts everyone."

There are also those who are always on the prowl for the best option. If you are in the habit of trying to secure a reservation at some of the better restaurants in town by making reservations at more than one establishment and then dining at the best one, you should be aware of the expression "You'll never eat lunch in this town again." If you don't intend to honor a reservation, follow through by calling the restaurant to cancel. Otherwise, you may find yourself on a restaurant blacklist.

Handling the Wait Staff

Bad service in any line of work can be disruptive. The key priority of a waiter is to serve with a smile. Congenial service can go far, and buffers any honest mishap. If you find yourself the victim of the waiter who'd rather be playing Carnegie Hall than serving your meal, my suggestion is, "Kill him with kindness." This trusted strategy of mine has put a few *wactors* (waiters who want to be actors) in their place.

The Zagats also recommend that you remain calm when a waiter isn't up to par, advising dissatisfied customers to call the manager. This is assuming that the restaurant in general is doing everything they can to make you happy. "If they're smart," says Tim Zagat, "they will offer to replace your dish. From your standpoint they're replacing your twenty-dollar entrée, but, from their side, they're replacing four dollars' worth of ingredients and making you happy." Customers may not realize how important it is to a restaurant to ensure your happiness. Restaurants are all too aware of the customer's power and recourse. In the case of unforgivably bad service, says Zagat, "You can always send a discriminating letter to the local restaurant reviewer, or, perhaps more damaging, you can take your business elsewhere."

Attracting the Waiter's Attention

To alert the nearest waiter without making a spectacle, just subtly raise your hand when he or she is in close proximity. If this doesn't attract some attention, politely ask a busboy or another restaurant staff person to contact the waiter for you.

Reading the Menu

On an à la carte menu, each item is priced separately. Often the entrée on an à la carte menu will include potatoes or rice; the vegetable will be additional. On a prix fixe menu, the price includes appetizer, entrée, and dessert. A few restaurants provide menus without prices—only the names of dishes that are included—to everyone in the party except the host, who is given a menu that includes prices. The host is defined as the person responsible for paying the check.

Supplemental charges may appear on a menu of a better restaurant. A dish that contains exotic or pricey ingredients—caviar or truffles, for instance—will typically contain an added charge.

The Wine List

The wine steward (sommelier) or, if there is none, the captain will show the host the wine list. The host may defer to someone more knowledge-able about wines. If no one at the table is a connoisseur, the host may ask the steward to recommend a suitable wine. The host need not be embarrassed to ask for a modestly priced wine. If some diners order meat and others choose fish, they may all agree to drink a red, white, or rosé wine, or they may all order half-bottles of red and white.

The wine steward shows the bottle to the host before uncorking it, so that the host can read the label to be sure it is the wine he ordered. After opening the bottle, the wine steward may hand the cork to the host so that he can feel that it is strong. The host may also sniff the cork to be sure that it is free from any musty smell. The sommelier then pours a small amount of wine into the host's glass. The host tastes the wine and may smell its bouquet to be sure it's good. Another reason for pouring the wine first in the host's glass is so that the host will receive any bits of cork that may have been floating at the top of the bottle. If the host is still sipping a cocktail when the wine is brought to the table, he may ask someone else at the table to taste the wine so that the waiter won't have to wait and the guests won't be deprived from beginning their wine. During the meal the waiter refills the glasses, typically halfway. Guests should not have to pour the wine themselves.

Giving Your Order

The captain typically asks the women for their orders and then asks the men. The host's order is taken last. When the party is large, the captain asks for each person in turn for his order. If the menu is in a foreign language, or there are dishes that you are not certain of, ask the captain or the waiter to help you.

If a price is not available or you are curious about how much the special costs, it can be awkward to ask the price directly. It is best to assume that item is as much as the most expensive entrée on the menu.

Special Orders

Asking for a particular part of the meal to be "on the side" is not only big with Meg Ryan's character in *When Harry Met Sally*, but it's also a trait shared by finicky eaters everywhere. If there is nothing on the menu that seems appealing, or you require specific dietary constraints, it's always permissible to ask for a meal prepared to your specifications.

Don't be intimidated. Nina Zagat says that you should assume that the restaurant is on your side, willing to accommodate your needs no matter how bizarre they may be. "A good restaurant will be able to serve something that is available on the menu, just tailored to your specifications. It is absolutely expected. Some people have dietary restrictions and need less salt or fat," says Nina.

Discussing Your Diet

I don't know of a person who hasn't at one time or another tried to diet. While anyone is interested in tips for a good weight-loss plan, the details of a person's diet can become less appetizing when shared during a meal. Diets shouldn't become the main topic of conversation when being entertained at a restaurant.

Sharing Meals

Since, practically speaking, you can only ever order one entrée, sometimes part of the fun of dining out is getting to taste a bit of what someone else at the table has ordered. On such occasions, your neighbor should serve you a portion of his meal with a serving spoon onto an extra side dish.

There are also those who find it offensive to share a drinking glass, take a bite from someone's ice cream cone, or share a dish at a Chinese restaurant. No, these people do not have to talk this one out with a therapist—it's just their way. Be respectful and always ask first if your dinner companion would mind sharing a meal.

If your dinner companion is not accustomed to ordering a meal with the intent of sharing, it is presumptuous to assume that you can claim a taste of his meal. If you are the person who prefers not to share and someone asks you for a bite of your meal, you can say, "I am so hungry and don't know if this will even satisfy me. Should we order another entrée?"

Table Hopping

Walk into some local hot spots and it's like you've just walked into a wedding with so many familiar faces around. If someone approaches your table to say hello, keep the visit to a greeting. A person standing in the aisle may obstruct the flow of a restaurant or the duties of the restaurant staff. If that visitor has many juicy details that need to be shared, pull up an extra chair so that she can temporarily be seated. Introduce others to the raconteur only if you would like that person to join you for a moment. To refrain from introductions is a way of saying that this isn't the right time to visit.

If you see friends in a restaurant to whom you'd like to say hello, don't table-hop while they are eating. Wait until they have finished their meal and when the time is more conducive for an impromptu greeting.

No-Host Parties

When a group gathers at a restaurant or a club to entertain a special occasion, the person organizing the evening will usually corral the group via e-mail or an invitation. In order for it to be clear to everyone that the person orchestrating the event is not *paying* for the event, a follow-up call is necessary. The person organizing the event may say, "We are able to celebrate Tom's birthday so lavishly only if everyone can contribute to a portion of the entertainment."

Dining Alone

For the business traveler or the person who wants a quick bite after a late night at the office, it's common to dine out alone. The Zagats recommend places like sushi bars—hotel restaurants that generally serve solo travelers or even elegant restaurants that have a comfortable counter setup. However, a woman should think twice about dining alone in a bar, as she may quickly attract unwanted dinner companions.

If you are concerned about how you will appear when dining alone, you may allay self-consciousness by making the meal a personal extravagance. This is an opportune time to study the menu and wine list since there is no one to hurry you. And, as Robert Morley once said, "No man is lonely while eating spaghetti; it requires too much attention."

The Tab

The person who asks the waiter to bring the bill is the one expected to pay it. To avoid any quarrels settling the tab, an appropriate strategy is to leave your credit card with the waiter beforehand. For a group that dines out together, usually the savvy guest with a head for numbers crunches the appropriate figure, including the tip, and divides the total among all parties—usually an even number. Each guest can then either offer credit card or cash or instruct the waiter accordingly. I feel it's best to not get into the "who ordered what" strategy of dividing the bill, since that's very past century.

Past Century/ Present Century

Today, single people have their own rights, largely expressed through their financial independence. When dining out with a couple, a single person—man or woman—should be prepared to pay his or her share of the meal. Single women were once expected to be treated by men, but today, with so many working women out there, it is assumed that they can cover their portion of the bill.

When Someone Doesn't Pay His or Her Share

I'd hate to assume that anyone who didn't pay her share of the bill would do so intentionally. Possibly he or she only had a credit card, and cash was the only acceptable form of payment, or the person was away from the table when the bill was handled. Regardless of the reason, you may be too embarrassed to ask for the money. If this is the case, you can drop the person a note or e-mail:

Dear Matt,
Your share of the dinner meal at Ferrier was $45. Had a great time, hope to do it again soon.

Tipping

The standard tip is 15 to 20 percent. This is your report card to the waiter on how you rate his service. It's customary, and usually expected, to include tips on your credit card, but a cash tip is always appreciated.

A sommelier should receive 15 percent of the wine bill if he was especially helpful in your selection. Bartenders receive 15 to 20 percent of your drink order if you had a cocktail before being seated. If drinks at the bar are rolled over onto your bill, you should settle the bartender's tip beforehand. Checkroom attendants receive upward of one dollar per item. A valet should receive two to five dollars for returning your car.

"If you want a special table or request additional services, such as champagne or dessert as a surprise for a birthday guest, tip the maître d'. If you are especially pleased with the service and it's an establishment that you frequent often, tip the maître d' when you leave, otherwise it is assumptive. You should also take the business card of that maître d' so you can call him on the next time," says Amy Sacco, owner of Lot 61. "Tipping doesn't necessarily have to be cash—it can be a thank-you note or a gift," adds Amy.

DO'S

1 Do confirm a dinner date with a friend on the day of the planned dinner.

2 Do be cordial on the phone when making a dinner reservation.

3 Do complain to the manager if your meal or service was unacceptable.

4 Do ask the steward for his wine recommendation.

5 Do customize your order to your dietary needs.

6 Do dine alone at an appropriate restaurant.

DON'TS

1) Don't make reservations at more than one establishment unless you are sure to cancel those you don't intend to honor.

2) Don't lose control if you are given bad service.

3) Don't discuss your diet at the table.

4) Don't presume that you can have a taste of your dining companion's meal.

5) Don't table-hop while others are still eating.

6) Don't feel obligated to pay for the person who didn't contribute to the bill.

DINING RIGHT QUIZ

After making a reservation, you should:
  A. Call to confirm that day.
  B. Call to confirm a few days before.
  C. Let the restaurant know if there will be any changes in number of guests.
  D. Any of the above.

ANSWER: D

In trying to attract a waiter's attention, you should:
  A. Wait until he checks on your table.
  B. Subtly raise your hand when he is in close proximity.
  C. Get up from your table and locate him in the restaurant.
  D. Call out his name or "waiter."

ANSWER: B

On an à la carte menu:
  A. Food is served buffet style.
  B. Food is less expensive.
  C. The tip is included.
  D. Each item is priced separately.

ANSWER: D

A prix fixe menu includes:
  A. The entrée only.
  B. An appetizer, entrée, and dessert.
  C. All you can eat.
  D. None of the above.

ANSWER: B

A sommelier is:
   A. The person who hands out warm facecloths.
   B. The bathroom attendant.
   C. The violinist.
   D. The wine steward.
ANSWER: D

The wine list is given to:
   A. Everyone at the table.
   B. The guest of honor.
   C. The wine connoisseur.
   D. The host.
ANSWER: D

When inviting a group to a no-host party to celebrate a guest of honor, the organizer should:
   A. Foot the bill.
   B. Assume that everyone will contribute.
   C. Just pay for her own and the guest's portion and everyone else will pay their own share.
   D. Make clear the payment procedure before the dinner.
ANSWER: D

If a guest didn't contribute to the bill, you should:
   A. Ask the manager to handle it.
   B. Never dine out with that person again.
   C. Confront him at the restaurant.
   D. Drop him a polite note the next day.
ANSWER: D

Expert Advice

Daniel Boulud,
Executive Chef/Restaurateur

Dining Out Well

Daniel Boulud is the chef and owner of the heralded New York City restaurants Daniel and Café Boulud. His other endeavors include Feast & Fêtes, the exclusive catering department of Restaurant Daniel; his "Private Stock" line of Caspian caviar and Scottish smoked salmon; as well as a partnership with award-winning Pastry Chef Francois Payard of Payard Patisserie & Bistro. He has received outstanding culinary acclaim from leading restaurant critics, has written two cookbooks, and appears on many cooking shows.

It's not just the ability to cook a roasted beef tenderloin with celery root puree and black truffle sauce that awakens the senses of my patrons to sheer culinary delight—it's as important a job for me to be hospitable. A restaurant must have flexibility. However, a restaurant is certainly challenged by the forgetful guest. A guest's negligence in canceling a reservation, or even a simple late arrival, will throw off an entire night. A good restaurant will call the guest on the day of reservation as a reminder—this is primarily so a restaurant can be assured of the number of meals to prepare for that evening. Maintaining a smooth operation behind the kitchen door begins hours before the patrons even arrive. If there is a cancellation, a hostess can easily fill that spot.

Timing is everything when it comes to preparing a meal. For example, if a guest strays from the table the moment the food is being served, the entire meal could be compromised as a result. I once cooked beef tenderloin for the king of Spain, which he found to be a little too pink. Rather than have his dinner companions wait for his meal to come back, we served him a side dish to keep him sated so everyone else could enjoy their meals.

The pressure of cooking a meal for President Clinton, the first lady, and sixty guests was a real challenge. This was a four-course meal that needed to be served within forty-five minutes. As soon as a person finished his or her course, the plate was cleared. The guests were all so respectful of this precise rhythm and the fact that there was a schedule to honor, that we were not burdened by the lingering guest. That awareness on the part of the guests made the event easier and more pleasurable for everyone.

Being cognizant of the restaurant's needs allows the restaurant staff to better serve you. This includes arriving on time, being mindful of the rhythm of the kitchen, and being considerate of the other dinner guests.

DANIEL BOULUD'S MOST COURTEOUS CUSTOMER:

1. Orders a smart wine, considering selections from the sommelier as opposed to selecting a wine just because it's pricey.
2. Enjoys experimentation. The adventurous guest who is open to creativity chooses a dish because it is unique.
3. Isn't shy about requesting a special order. However, I don't always agree with a meal that's requested well done or overcooked. The courteous customer will defer to the chef's judgment on occasion.
4. Makes an effort to look nice, showing that she is dining for a special event.
5. Makes a future reservation *after* he's dined, not before he is seated. The ultimate compliment to the chef.

THAT'S ENTERTAINING

*E*ntertainment takes on many different forms, but whether you're hosting a cocktail party, a holiday, birthday, or anniversary bash, or having friends out to the country for a weekend, the objective is always the same—to have a good time.

Unfortunately, entertaining in today's fast-paced world can be a daunting task, especially if you work all day and find yourself with little time to make the preparations. Once upon a time, a host had the entire day to preside over her event. Today, that host has a job to go to and a salary to earn. How can one manage a career and entertain? The same way a socialite can balance a champagne flute in one hand and nibble on a sushi role in the other—with artful grace. Use the management and professional skills you've honed at the office to get a party off the ground without a hitch. A little planning, a few creative ideas, and the willingness to let others come to your aid, and you'll be the host or hostess with the mostess in no time.

What's to Entertain?

If you're accustomed to waiting for the holidays or a milestone event for excuses to throw a party, chances are you're missing out on engaging opportunities to be shared with good friends. It's more fun to throw an impromptu party. A party is also a festive way to expand your existing group and meet new people.

No Time to Entertain

Before you even think about turning your stove's dial, take a walk through a specialty food store or down your grocer's aisle. You'll find you can create a sumptuous menu without lifting a finger. New York City's Balducci's, for instance, has everything from caviar to cappuccino. Personally I love the cheese puffs that are available from my supermarket freezer. Today, hearty hors d'oeuvres may substitute for a full-blown meal. Substantial, and even quite elegant, shrimp, sushi roles, and crudités are not only easy to find already prepared but can also satisfy the most picky eater.

A few candles, some flowers delivered by your local florist, and the latest CDs are instant atmosphere makers. While there's no guarantee that your flambé will be a success, you can always count on your local bakery to have a delectable dessert that's sure to impress guests. No one needs to know who did the baking.

Brunch

Brunch is a great way to entertain simply and to make something special out of an ordinary Sunday. It is a limited and contained event with regard to time, and afterward, if the weather is good, guests can enjoy outdoor activities together. It's also less formal than a dinner, which makes the menu, setting, guest list, and planning more relaxed.

Tea

Even in a country of coffee drinkers, those dark, robust grounds never seem to have the same elegance and festiveness as tea. Alice was in quite a wonderland with her tea party, and Bostonians went down in history for theirs. And what little girl doesn't love to entertain her dolls and stuffed toys with her own version of high tea? In fact, the tea party is even more illustrious than the fables that are so familiar to us. The custom comes adorned with wedding gift bounties, elegant dress, and, ideally, a glorious day fit for the garden party circuit.

Afternoon tea began in the late 1700s when proper ladies, whose meals consisted of a big breakfast, small lunch, and late-evening snack, needed a boost to get them through the day's end.

Served between three and five o'clock, afternoon tea consists of a sampling of teas, finger sandwiches, scones, jam, light cakes, and, of course, great conversation in a relaxed atmosphere. High tea is served later in the day, usually after five o'clock, and is essentially a dinner with meats and bread.

I used to go to the Mayfair Regent to catch up with friends for an afternoon tea. It was a hidden secret in New York. The tables were far apart, the service was excellent, and the overall atmosphere provided such comfort that no one left without a big, silly grin. An acquaintance recently remarked that she considered teas to be dated. If elegant is dated, then I suppose that's so!

Cocktail Parties

Cocktail parties are a convenient venue for the after-work business event or for the host who wants to easily entertain a mix of interesting people without requiring too much time from anyone.

When inviting guests to your cocktail party, whether by written invitation, phone, or e-mail, specify not only what time the party begins but also what time it ends as well. Otherwise socialites may linger on until the next day. Not everyone who receives an invitation to a cocktail party will come, so if you want a fairly accurate estimate on how many guests to expect, include on the invitation an RSVP.

Your bar should be set up in an open area, since this will be a focal point where guests will gather. At a larger party, you may consider setting up more than one bar and having waiters serve drinks. You need not offer every imaginable drink; the basics will suffice—scotch, vodka, rum, red and white wine along with the mixers (orange, cranberry, and tomato juices, and tonic water). The nonalcoholic mixers will tide over the guests who won't be drinking.

It's easier to throw a cocktail party in a contained space where people are automatically thrown together, but don't jam them together—make sure guests have enough room to circulate easily. Move any large pieces of furniture that might get in the way.

Personalized Parties

Romance, Murder Mysteries, and the Call of the Wild—no, this is not a lineup for new cable channels, but some ideas for theme parties. Rather than host an evening where guests can expect simply a good meal and, ideally, interesting conversation, some entertainers raise the stakes of an evening by adding some intrigue.

For example, author Lauren Purcell hosts an annual wine-tasting party. Though wine tasting may conjure up the image of a gathering of wine snobs or the likes of TV's Frasier and Niles Crane, her gathering is quite the contrary. "I will invite anyone who is interesting—from the aficionados to the beer drinkers. There will be guests who have never ordered a bottle of wine with dinner and people with impressive wine collections—yet they all have fun within the group."

Dinner Party Gifts

Yes, this is not a misprint, I really am saying that receiving flowers can be an onus. When throwing a dinner party, flowers are a distraction from my priorities. I have to step away, find a vase, and attend to the arrangement. All this takes me away from other matters. Gifts, such as a bottle of wine or specialty foods, are a thoughtful gesture but not necessary. Instead a note, follow-up call, or any postsentiment that expresses your thanks is always polite.

Arrivals

The fifteen-minute-late standard is acceptable for a dinner party; in fact, your host probably expects it. However, dinner should not be put off for a few late stragglers. There's no reason why everyone else should be put out. Guests should be cognizant that the evening cannot be set back due to their late arrival. If you are held up in traffic, at the office, etc., be sure to call and assure your host she should begin without you.

Uninvited Guests

First, why anyone would attempt to crash a party is beyond me. It takes a strangely confident person to make an appearance at an event where she isn't wanted. The uninvited guest is a hanger-on and presents a difficult situation for the host. If there is service at the party, the host could have the help to ask the person to leave. If there is no help at the party, you could say, "I am so sorry but there is not enough food prepared for an extra guest."

If an invited guest has brought an additional person without covering it with the host beforehand, and you are not prepared to entertain the added guest, then you should tell the invited guest this and leave it to him or her to handle the situation. If a houseguest would like to invite someone for dinner, he needs to check with the host. The guest is responsible for the additional person and should therefore make sure the dynamic will be conducive. If it's a seated dinner, be prepared that there are only so many seats and that you may well be refused.

Mingling

There are those who can work a room like a politician at an event padded with campaign donors. Others find the process tedious and mildly superficial, a good book and warm bath being strong temptations for a quick exit. If social skills aren't your forte, lean on your host for a friendly nudge. It's the host's responsibility to make sure that everyone is introduced and drinks are filled. Be certain not to monopolize the host's time, however; as congenial as she may appear to be, you do not want to interfere with her hosting duties. A good introduction usually entails a quick brief on everyone's bios. Shared interests between guests usually makes for a handy conversation opener. (See Chapter II, the "Introductions" section.) Otherwise there's always sports, politics, and the latest series on FOX to discuss.

Yawning

The best advice on yawning I've seen comes from George Washington himself, who once said, "If you . . . Yawn, do it not Loud but Privately and Speak not in your Yawning but put Your handkerchief or Hand before your face and turn aside." Thus proving that George had more talents than just pulling a country together.

If your yawn interrupts a conversation, apologize by blaming it on lack of sleep even if boredom is the reason. If you're mired in tedious conversation, an obvious yawn will do nothing to extricate you from that conversation, nor will it make the person speaking a more interesting conversationalist. So there is nothing to be gained by yawning to make a point.

When caught with a conversationally challenged acquaintance, try to enlist a passerby into the discussion, preferably one to whom you don't owe a favor, since hijacking him will add another to the list. Then you can make an excuse for a quick getaway by paraphrasing Robert Browning: "But, my dear fellow, this is too bad. I am monopolizing you."

A Conversation with Someone Older

Who doesn't have the wrinkled auntie Agnes who sits aside during holiday celebrations, draped in a woolen blanket, speaking endlessly of the good old days? In my family, unbeknownst to Great-auntie, of course, all the children were assigned specified time segments in which to spend indulging her and her signature antiquated stories.

Younger people often find it difficult to speak with someone several generations older. They may be uncertain how to initiate a conversation or they may fear that they have nothing to say that will hold the elder's interest.

It is true that older people should always be treated with special consideration. Youngsters should learn the importance of being courteous while minding not to become patronizing when merely trying to be respectful. To begin a conversation, the younger person should speak clearly and audibly, since the older person may be hard of hearing. She could begin the discussion with topics she knows best—school, friends, social activities. While these may appear obvious choices to the child, these very topics are precisely what may interest the elder person. This is their contact to the youth and social situation happenings of today. The younger person may also find the experiences of his elder to be fascinating. It can be exciting to learn from someone who has experienced life.

A Conversation with Someone Younger

When confronted with a small child, an adult may become flustered in how to approach this tiny person. Children, even small ones, have distinct personalities, likes, and dislikes. They react to new people in much the same way an adult would. Therefore, those who aren't used to being around children will get along very well with them as long as they act as though they are meeting an adult.

"I speak to my son Liam, who is six, in a regular tone, and those who meet him will get more of a response if they do the same," says my friend Timmy Stanton. You shouldn't have to condescend to a small child or attempt to ingratiate yourself. It is known that horses can sense the fear of a human. I've always thought that little children have the same ability. If you feel out of place among small children, don't overcompensate and camouflage the feeling; it won't work.

If you'd like to make a connection with a toddler, he will become an instant friend if you will grant him a peek inside your handbag or briefcase. And don't forget that small children, just like us all, love a sincere compliment.

Conversations with Someone Who Has Different Interests

I have a friend, Sophie, whose uncle is a brain surgeon, literally. While she finds it difficult to speak with him for fear that her intellectual capacity will not be up to par, I've always found her insecurities to be unfounded. At a dinner party where her uncle was in attendance, Sophie spoke about her passion for scuba diving and a recent expedition she went on in Costa Rica. She also discussed fashion and the art of throwing an event, as she is in the public relations field. Her uncle looked to Sophie with studied curiosity. What Sophie may have not realized is that her uncle appreciated the exposure that she had given him of her world, one that is foreign to his. Which proves that everyone has something interesting to say.

Guests and Seating

The seating arrangement is another aspect of entertaining that has thankfully been liberated from the formalities of my mother's time. She would never have set a table that wasn't even—having an equal ratio of males to females. In the twenty-first century, worrying about a finite number of guests takes the serendipity out of the affair, which now-adays is more about the mix than the match. Some of the best dinner parties are not about the meals and table setting, it's about meeting an assortment of people—with varied interests, careers—and becoming enlightened.

However, some planning, along with a little common sense with re-gard to seating, can go a long way toward setting a dynamic of the table. Unless it's a new relationship, avoid putting a couple together. It's also fun to spice things up by playing matchmaker. It's always fun putting friends together who could possibly make a romantic connection. If the event is larger and there are many tables to assign, seating couples with other cou-ples helps alleviate the pressure of networking. Orchestrating bigger parties presents its own host of tricky concerns—you'd have to be a therapist with a Ouija board to assemble a perfect plan. There will always be those partic-ular personalities that will become offended by being placed at the "left-over" table. For one party I hosted at a New York City hotel, with almost three hundred people to seat, rather than being assured of having a few guests disappointed by their table, I arranged alphabetically. And, in this in-stance, it was a success.

The Creative Table Setting

While bone-white china, polished silver, and the flicker of candlelight pre-sents an elegant setting, personal touches such as pareos (colorful wraps) that masquerade as a tablecloth or a centerpiece of seasonal fruit and ex-otic leaves have their own distinctive aura. The table's setting need not be a venue to showcase your wedding registries, but can be as creative and daz-zling as the main course. Just keep in mind that the setting, notably the centerpiece, shouldn't distract from dinner conversation. (See Chapter III for more on the formal table setting.)

The Menu

Unless it's a holiday where traditional foods dictate what to serve, cook what you enjoy. Attempt a new recipe you snipped from a magazine or prepare your surefire specialty. The other route? Call for help and leave the cooking to the professionals.

The responsibility of the gracious guest is to keep an open stomach. Choosing from a selection of courses as if from a dinner menu is presumptuous. For those who have dietary restrictions due to religion, health, or a finicky palate, it would be sensible to eat beforehand. Adding to the host's responsibilities is like asking your supervisor to finish your paperwork so you can leave the office early.

If there's still nothing offered that you find edible, do what the kids do and mix the food around your plate—mashed potatoes always provides an excellent hiding place for those dreaded Brussels sprouts.

If you are serving hors d'oeuvres for a cocktail party, simple fare such as a cheese platter, crudités, or sushi will do nicely. Whatever you serve, make sure that it can be handled with nothing more than a cocktail napkin and toothpick. A guest with a full plate in one hand and drink in the other can not only be a hazard to your white couch, but to himself and other guests.

Dinner Music

My father always said that dinner music prohibits conversation. Even if he was hosting a dinner dance, the music never began until after the meal was finished. This is one of those childhood rules I have grown used to. Nevertheless, many find music during dinner pleasurable—some even say it aids in digestion. Indeed, dinner music is not a contemporary phenomenon. Mozart wrote divertimentos for his friends' garden parties. Whatever your pleasure, just make sure that it doesn't drown out your mealtime companions' voices.

Dinner Conversation

It is up to the host to set the conversation at dinner, particularly when there is no discussion in action. While some may find it a chore to keep a conversation interesting, others revel in the opportunity to discuss themselves. This is also why an attention to seating is key. At one party I hosted, I seated Barbara Walters—whose business is to ask questions—next to a savvy conversationalist. His knack for bringing out the personal, unexpected side of any dinner partner was especially impressive when he turned the tables on Barbara and said, "Let's not talk about me but rather *you*." Barbara then gave an exclusive to some very personal questions and was probably relieved that someone else was asking the questions for a change.

While it's also enjoyable to fall into a comfortable conversation with the person seated next to you, it's important to be aware of those seated near you. Avoid returning to those catty school-yard days when the class snobs excluded others from an open discussion. Listen to other table companions' conversations and jump in when you have something to contribute.

The Awkward Pause

Who hasn't felt the panic set in when faced with an excruciatingly long lull in the conversation? Rather than pray for any interruption to save you, it's always a good idea to have a stash of reserve questions. Following are some topics other than work, the weather, and politics to ask the person sitting next to you:

- Do you spend most of your time in the city?
- What's the latest cinema gossip?
- How do you know the host?
- Where will you be spending the holidays?

After Dinner

Offering to clear the table at a party where there is professional help is obtrusive. Look to the nature of the gathering—if it's just a small group of close friends for a casual dinner, it's only natural that everyone will volunteer to share the cleaning responsibility. At a more formal dinner, it's really not necessary or desirable for the guests to help in the kitchen. As a general rule, I feel that it's always proper to make the offer, which can be as simple as saying "May I assist?" or "Can I help?" This allows your host the option of declining your courteous offer.

Coffee, Tea—You're Free to Leave

When coffee and/or tea is served, it's the signal for the end of the meal. You may consider moving your guests to another room, which allows them the opportunity to mingle with those they didn't get to speak to at the table. Also, it's nice to be able to stretch one's legs and not be confined to a dining room chair. Since coffee can be a long affair, anyone who wishes to go home at this point is perfectly free to do so.

Departures

I have one friend who gauges the success of her parties by how late her guests stay. I don't find this necessary. Very often people would stay if they could but work, families, or personal responsibilities compete with a late-night social gathering. Once one guest makes an exit, the others usually follow close behind. However, for the evenings that lapse well beyond the extended curfew, it's always handy to have some bagels and morning coffee available.

DO'S

1 Do entertain whenever the mood moves you.

2 Do organize a brunch if you want to entertain casually.

3 Do call your host if you are going to be late.

4 Do treat older people with special consideration.

5 Do be creative when setting the table.

6 Do serve a variety of foods when selecting the menu for a dinner party.

DON'TS

① Don't feel obliged to prepare the entire menu without assistance.

② Don't forget to include the time your cocktail party ends on the invitation.

③ Don't feel that you have to be a wine connoisseur at a wine-tasting party.

④ Don't play dinner music so loudly that it drowns out conversation.

⑤ Don't panic if there is a lull in the conversation.

⑥ Don't gauge the success of a party just by how long it lasts.

THAT'S ENTERTAINING QUIZ

High tea is served:
   A.   At breakfast.
   B.   In the midafternoon.
   C.   After five o'clock.
   D.   After dinner.
ANSWER: C

The bar at a cocktail party should be set up:
   A.   In a contained space.
   B.   Where the guests arrive.
   C.   In the kitchen.
   D.   Near a sink.
ANSWER: A

An inappropriate dinner party gift is:
   A.   Nothing.
   B.   Flowers.
   C.   Cookies or candy.
   D.   Alcohol.
ANSWER: B

If you unexpectedly yawn in the middle of a conversation:
   A.   Blame it on lack of sleep.
   B.   Quickly find someone new to speak with.
   C.   Ignore it.
   D.   None of the above.
ANSWER: A

A table seating should have:
  A. An equal ratio of males to females.
  B. Men and women only seated next to the opposite sex.
  C. An even number of people.
  D. None of the above.
ANSWER: D

A guest does not have to help clear the table:
  A. When there is professional help.
  B. When he or she did not eat anything.
  C. If he or she helped set the table.
  D. None of the above.
ANSWER: A

Expert Advice

Colin Cowie, Entertainment Enterpriser

Easy Entertaining

Colin Cowie is the founder of Colin Cowie Lifestyle, an event-planning and catering company in Los Angeles and New York. Colin has been the mastermind of some of Hollywood's most spectacular parties for celebrities.

Colin is a spokesperson and designer for Lenox China, a contributing editor to InStyle *magazine, and the host of his own cable television show,* Everyday Elegance *on the Romance Classics channel. He has appeared regularly on* The Oprah Winfrey Show, Good Morning America, Entertainment Tonight, *and* E! Television. *Colin has also been featured in* USA Today, *the* Los Angeles Times, Biography *magazine,* Brides *magazine,* People *magazine,* InStyle *magazine,* Chicago Daily Tribune, Southern California Bride, NY Bride, Connecticut Bride, Florida Bride, *and* Chicago Bride.

We are living in a new century where we are no longer required to peel, chop, and sauté, or spend hours in the kitchen preparing for guests. Today's savvy entertainer is someone who is resourceful. No longer are you measured by whether or not the meal is made from scratch—you get no medals! In a world where we have almost twenty-four-hour access to prepared food and decorations, we can put any party together with style, grace, and elegance at a moment's notice.

Therefore, the question is never *can* I throw a party but rather *what kind* of party should I throw? If you enjoy setting a nice table and selecting fine wines but find the whole kitchen experience daunting, then create a list of great places or sources to help you with the details. Know where you can buy good quality food, possibly from your favorite restaurant, or have your favorite stone crabs sent overnight from Miami. A smart host or hostess is one who is glued to her guests, not chained to the kitchen. If you are the person who has knowledge of the kitchen and the desire to cook, then design a menu that allows you to do all of the preparation in advance so you can be a presence at the table.

When it comes to setting the table, when it comes to style, we are all masters. Gone are the days where the table has to be set with matching crystal, china, and silver. It's much more interesting to mix and match different patterns, styles, and shapes from different eras. Mix your family heirlooms with museum pieces and flea market finds. The end result will be a table that oozes personality and gives a window into a host's sense of style.

The responsibility of the guests is to make an effort to converse at the table, make sure never to use a cell phone at the party, to follow the lead of your host, and eat with impeccable table manners. Remember, the ultimate goal of the dinner party is the enjoyment and pleasure of other people's company in a stylish setting.

CHAPTER VI

THE
HOUSEGUEST

*A*waiting the arrival of a houseguest can feel a lot like beginning a new job; always there's a mix of excitement and fear. Inviting a guest to your home, however, shouldn't be a job. Setting some basic guidelines at the onset is your insurance against dealing with a difficult situation later on. Then you may freely enjoy the added company, and, who knows, you may never want your visitor to leave—then again . . .

The Good Guest

A great gift in a Tiffany blue box doesn't automatically grant the invited guest free range of his host's home. While housewarming gifts are always a generous token, a guest should first and foremost be accommodating to a friend's hospitality. Make yourself useful around the house when the time is right; watch carefully and you'll pick up the signals. For instance, wait for your host to initiate the washing up after dinner and then clear up naturally. Or, if your host attends to the gardening, you may volunteer to assist. In general you should always ask if there is any way that you can be of help.

However, be mindful not to volunteer for things that you are not skilled in doing. If you've never before prepared lasagna, for example, and are asked to make the sauce, you should suggest that you would be better suited to making the salad. The host will welcome your honesty far more than an inedible entrée.

Gift Ideas to Give to the Host

Wine

Specialty foods that can be served over the weekend

Pies or homemade desserts

Picture frames (send with photographs you took over the weekend)

Candles

Coffee table books

House Rules

Here's my dependable list of rules to follow when entertaining houseguests:

1. Establish what time you expect your guests to arrive and, just as important, when they are expected to leave.
2. Once they've arrived, make your guests feel at home. Allow them to get settled in their rooms. Leave some spontaneous signs of welcome. A warm towel to dry off with, for example. (Heating towels in the dryer takes less than a minute.) A hungry traveler always appreciates drinks and a snack set on a tray.
3. A host is entitled to his or her idiosyncrasies, and so is a guest. All particulars should be addressed in the beginning of the stay, otherwise it's catty to assume rules as you go along. If a host doesn't like a guest foraging through the refrigerator or if a guest devotes an hour of the day to yoga, these things should be cleared at the outset.

4. Your home is not boot camp. So rather than impose your own agenda—or be a slave to theirs—offer a selection of activities that will keep everyone happily occupied. Perhaps a visit to the local destination points—a vineyard, antiquing, or a day at the beach, for example. If your guests do not have a car, provide a schedule of public transportation or, if available, offer an extra car or bicycles.

5. Time and freedom are a luxury for any houseguest. A general rule that works for me is to allow guests to spend the day as they please. The one stipulation should be the time of dinner. For example, be clear that cocktails will be at 7:30 P.M. and dinner will be served at 8:00 P.M.

6. Guests should not only keep their room and belongings tidy, they should assist their host with any household work as much as possible. Don't be taken aback when your host has some weeding and light yard work for you to do. Painting the house? That may be overboard for room and board.

7. For the guest who doesn't offer to help, I don't consider it rude to enlist him.

8. At the end of a visit, guests should leave their room and bath-
    room as clean as it was when they arrived. They should ask their
    host if she would like them to strip their beds. A host should
    have cleaning products and linen baskets available to her guests.

The Morning Routine

Some of us are morning people, and for others, the only pep we want first
thing in the morning is from a cup of coffee. It's best to come clean with
one's morning routine from the start. The first person up may want to
make a bagel and coffee run—a gesture always welcomed by the late risers.
If a group decides to begin the day while others are still asleep, a note
should be left regarding the plan in case the others want to join you later.

For those who like to sleep well into the afternoon, save the extended
slumbers when you are not a guest or a host. It's not polite to snooze the
day away, especially when the host may have something planned.

The host should never sleep too late. Recently I spent the weekend at
my friend Bob's house. Bob is usually a gracious, relaxed host. However,
one morning a few of us woke early and began to prepare breakfast. Suddenly Bob stormed into the kitchen and berated us for waking him up.

Needless to say, Bob overreacted. When more than three people are
sharing a house, there is no need for territorial behavior and short tem-
pers. Had it been my house, I would have been delighted that my guests
were enjoying themselves so thoroughly without my help. Then again, I'm
an early riser. I can't say I'd be so forgiving if awakened in the middle of
the night. Naturally, it's best to avoid any confrontation and try to abide by
people's requests within reason.

If It Doesn't Belong to You, It Doesn't Belong to You

I love surprises, except when I am responsible for paying for them. Recently I discovered that a guest made a seventy-two-minute call from my

home in New York to Utah. For that amount, I might as well have splurged on his airfare so that he could visit his phone mate in person. Apparently this rule, despite how obvious it may seem, needs to be reiterated—don't ever use the phone to make long distance calls, borrow anything without asking, or assume that as a guest you are entitled to your host's belongings.

Naturally, food in the kitchen, linens, and bathroom items should be available for a guest's needs and a host should direct the guest to these items. A courteous guest should always ask before using something. One guest of mine borrowed a book from my library but was unable to finish it by the end of the weekend. He even went so far as to try to find a copy for himself at the local bookstore only to discover that it was out of print. He then politely asked me if he could borrow the book and return it when he was finished. With such exemplary manners, how could I not loan it to him? The following week he returned the book with a note and a copy of another book that he thought I would enjoy. That's a houseguest who is welcome anytime.

The Extended Guest

For the guest who is staying longer than a weekend, it is essential to establish a set of rules from the beginning. Your visitor needs to understand your lifestyle, schedule, and routine so that you are not inconvenienced. Long-term guests should maintain their own agenda so that life as you commonly know it will not be compromised.

Upon arrival, the guest should be given a tour of your home. This is also a good opportunity for them to learn where the linens, tableware, and toiletries are kept. Equally as important, if there is no household help to tidy up after your guests, it would also be beneficial to direct them to the washer and dryer. Sharing in the expenses and household work is reasonable, since the host should not be put out financially or burdened with extra housework.

Inviting a relative stranger into your home for more than five days only works on reality television. Who wants the added tension in your own home?

Unexpected Guests

A close friend who casually drops by at my summer home, knowing that I'd probably be playing with my grandchildren, would be an unexpected but welcome treat. However, when a friend randomly buzzes me at my apartment in Manhattan, I have to wonder what strange force possessed her to do such an odd thing. City living tends to be more formal, regimented. Therefore an unexpected visitor could be disruptive. In the country, where the atmosphere is more casual, dropping by is part of the social scene. There always seems to be at least one house that has an open-door policy. Whether in the city or the country, you can alleviate any stress on your friends by following one general rule: Call first. This allows the hosts time to quickly make themselves and their home presentable.

If you've been interrupted by unannounced visitors and don't feel you can send them away, ask your guests to make themselves comfortable in another room (it's fine to treat a drop-in informally) and finish up whatever you were doing if it can't be postponed.

Time Shares

While sharing summer rentals is an increasingly popular trend, things can often go from fun to fiasco before you even reach July Fourth. Similar to the rules that apply to the houseguest, all issues with your housemates should be handled in the beginning. The most common summer share debacle involves finances. Before committing to a summer house or any time share, find out how much your share is, if it includes expenses, and the guest privileges. Dealing with the "Who had the Diet Coke and who ordered the extra appetizer?" scenario is difficult enough when allocating a restaurant bill; "Who made a long-distance call?" and "Who took the longest hot shower?" is almost impossible to itemize. With household expenses, I think it's best to split each bill evenly. Cooking and cleaning is another heated issue. It's usually best to have an open fridge in these situations. If you are particular about your bowl of Frosted Flakes in the morning, do the college dorm-living thing and mark your packages accordingly.

Weekly maid service is always a good idea, since, in situations of group living, it's inevitable that there will be a few Oscars to one Felix. And, try not to take up all of the hot water.

Pets

For many, leaving a pet behind for a weekend away at a friend's can be a difficult parting. Check with the host beforehand to see if your pet is also welcome. Your hosts may actually appreciate the added company. However, keep in mind that no matter how much you may love little Cocoa, other people may not love his slobbery kisses or his begging for scraps from the table. Cats have a tendency to jump into a stranger's lap, which may startle some people.

It's up to you to control your pet—tearing apart the flower bed or jumping in the pool (as a certain springer spaniel once did in my home), is cause for immediate banishment. You should make any amends to the host and relegate the animal to a place where it cannot cause further disruption.

> ## Past Century/ Present Century
>
> *Socks are in. While traipsing around one's home in socks has always been commonplace in Asian cultures, to ask someone to remove his shoes when inviting him into your home once appeared a bizarre gesture in America. It's now all the rage. Whether it's the customized flooring, preserving the home's upkeep, or eliminating dirt and grime, many homeowners are establishing a no-shoe policy. Always be prepared to put your best foot forward and wear nice socks.*

DO'S

❶ Do offer your assistance to your host at a suitable time.

❷ Do leave a note as to where you will be if you are leaving the house and the host is not available.

❸ Do quietly entertain yourself when there is an absentee host.

4 Do allow your guests time to get settled in after they arrive.

5 Do prepare a list or selection of activities that your guest may be interested in.

6 Do assist your host with any light household work.

7 Do call first before dropping by.

DON'TS

1. Don't offer to help in a task at which you are not skilled.
2. Don't sleep through the entire day.
3. Don't wake up the host if she made it clear not to.
4. Don't restrict a guest or host from engaging in idiosyncrasies.
5. Don't feel it impertinent to ask a guest for some assistance.

HOUSEGUEST QUIZ

The first one up should:
   A. Wake the others.
   B. Begin his normal routine.
   C. See if there is anything that can be done around the house.
   D. Any of the above.

ANSWER: C

When inviting a guest to stay, the host should:
   A. Make it clear when the guests should arrive and leave.
   B. Be flexible with the duration of the stay.
   C. Not entertain someone for more than three days.
   D. None of the above.

ANSWER: A

If a guest does not have a car, the host should:
   A. Provide a schedule of public transportation.
   B. Offer an available car or bicycle.
   C. Take the guest where he has to go if it's not disruptive.
   D. Any of the above.

ANSWER: D

Guests should spend the day:
   A. Doing as they are instructed.
   B. Having been given a selection of ideas, have the freedom to do as they please.
   C. Going along with their own schedule.
   D. Cleaning and assisting with the upkeep of the home.

ANSWER: B

A host entertaining a long-term guest should:

    A. Allow his guest to do as she pleases.

    B. Establish guidelines so everyone can maintain their own lifestyles.

    C. Entertain as he would a weekend guest.

    D. Ask for rent.

ANSWER: B

Expert Advice

André Balazs, Hotelier

Coming Over

André Balazs is one of the leading hoteliers of our time. He is president of the W and The Standard hotels, a group of twenty-two sophisticated urban hotels in cities from New York to Sydney. He is also the owner of The Mercer Hotel in New York, the Chateau Marmont in Hollywood, Sunset Beach Hotel on Shelter Island, and a new super-luxury hotel now being built in Soho. Mr. Balazs has also created, owned, and operated numerous restaurants and nightclubs, such as M.K. and Nica's at the Stanhope, in both New York and Los Angeles.

Mr. Balazs has been a trustee of the New York Academy of Art for over ten years and is a member of the National Arts Club and the University Club. Mr Balazs is a graduate of Cornell University's College Scholar program and holds an M.S. from Columbia University's joint MBA/Journalism program. He is married to Katie Ford, CEO of Ford Models, one of the world's largest modeling agencies, and has two daughters, ages eleven and seven.

An invitation to friends for a weekend spent at your home is the warmest, most sincere gift one can offer. Maintaining the familial atmosphere requires little work, probably less work than following a more regimented structure.

At our home in Shelter Island, New York there is no distinction between regular family members and the weekend guest. This dynamic is key to maintaining an undisturbed household. Our guest is essentially a member of the family—which is the key.

Whether a weekend is filled with back-to-back activities or comfortable days surrounded by food and relaxation, there are always enjoyable moments to be shared. In the summer months, our family hosts guests more frequently. Since we are already accustomed to an active schedule—sports, water games, the beach—these are the kinds of activities we share with our guests. These kinds of routines are more about the fun than the performance. You are not really entertaining in the formal sense. It's more of a casual affair that makes for a comfortable weekend.

The trick is not to make too much of having a weekend guest. As a hotel manager, I am all too familiar with the demands of formal hospitality. With weekend guests, my attitude is to avoid any impersonal constraints when it comes to your home. A home shouldn't have the feel of a hotel. A houseguest should be able to experience your life with you. What's the point of presenting a false image—otherwise they might as well stay at a hotel. Informality is what real family life, my family's life, is about.

The friends we invite are those who will ease nicely into the spirit of our home. Some friends can blend into our schedule seamlessly while others may not. You want to be able to see them over the breakfast table and enjoy their company before you go to bed.

On the flip side, when I am a guest, I feel most comfortable when the host feels comfortable. It's always about comfort and establishing that personal hospitality where a family's personality begins to shine through.

CHAPTER VII

CORRESPONDENCE

*L*ike a sparkling diamond in a mountain of coal, the handwritten note is a precious jewel among the mountain of bills and junk mail—all the more so in today's fast paced, computer-generated world. It can be saved and read again. Everything from the handwriting to the stationery and special delivery keep the art of letter writing a treasured and timely sentiment. Letters should never become past century. They are also the only way to send a proper thank-you note or condolence message.

Business Letters

A business letter must contain your contact information so that the receiver can reciprocate your query, the date so he knows when your request was submitted, and the recipient's address. For example:

Jason E. Snyder
Agenda Webcast
110 Mercer Street
New York, New York 10011

December 11, 2001

Mr. Arthur Jordan
Jordan Capital
500 Park Avenue
New York, New York 10021

Dear Mr. Jordan:

I am interested in speaking with you in regards to investment opportunities with my company, Agenda Webcast, an Internet site and media company that I started three years ago that enables users to locate entertainment venues by geographical region via *www.agenda.com* and a supplemental biweekly magazine.

Enclosed you will find a financial history of the company along with press clippings and a copy of the most recent publication. You can contact me at (212) 555-1515 or e-mail me at *jsnyder@agenda.com*. I look forward to speaking with you further.

Sincerely,

Jason E. Snyder
President

It's also advisable to send a business letter on company letterhead or personal stationery so that the recipient will have all your information. Letterhead also allows you to conserve space and keep the look cleaner. Naturally, all business letters need to be grammatically correct. "One spelling mistake on a query letter or résumé, and these candidates don't get called in for an interview," says Michael Moaba, Vice Chairman of M. Shanken Communications.

The expression "Less is more" is not only a great tip on how to accessorize, it also applies to writing. The contents of a letter should get your main points across quickly. No one likes to meander through garbled sentences, especially when there is a stack of other letters that need to be attended to.

Addressing People

A formal letter should include Mr., Mrs., Ms., or Miss before the recipient's name. The following are guidelines on what is the appropriate title for whom:

Girls and young women

Though *Miss* may seem a tad past century, I've always found it to be a classic way to address a young lady.

Married women

A married woman can be addressed "Mrs. Jerry Pierce," "Mrs. Kate Pierce," "Ms. Kate Pierce," or by her maiden name if she has not taken her husband's name. If the letter is being sent to both her and her husband, and she has kept or hyphenated her name, both names should be addressed on the envelope. "Mrs. Kate Pierce" is the standard way to address a divorcée.

A widow

For a woman whose husband is deceased, she should still be referred to by her married name, "Mrs. John Schwartz."

Doctors and judges

If you know doctors socially, it is customary to speak to them on a first-name basis. It is also acceptable to address their letters this way.

A married woman doctor and her husband should be addressed as "Dr. Liza Atwood and Mr. Ethan Atwood." If both husband and wife are doctors, you could simply write "the Drs. Atwood." The same rule applies to judges.

Academic degrees

A PhD in an academic environment should be addressed "Dr. Leonard Stone." For a personal letter, it is not necessary.

Salutation and Closing

If you are on a first-name basis with the person to whom you are sending the letter, then you should address the person that way. If it is a business contact whom you have never met, then address that person by his or her formal name. It's presumptuous in such cases to assume a first-name basis—especially if the letter is a sales pitch. If you've met the person a few times, you should still address him by his full name until you become more familiar with this contact. After a few meetings or regular phone contact, then you are justified to be more casual.

"Sincerely," "Best," "Best regards," and "Yours truly" are all acceptable forms of closing for a business letter.

Thank-You Notes

The sooner you write a thank-you note, the more lively and spontaneous the note will be. A thank-you note should be sent within a week from your receipt of the sentiment. With the exception of thank-yous for wedding presents, which are generally written on formal stationery, you may use informal paper. Anyone would be pleased to receive a thank-you letter regardless of the type of gesture. However, there are certain instances when it is obligatory. They are as follows:

- After receiving a present by mail.
- After a weekend visit.
- After receiving a gift if you're in the hospital.
- Wedding presents.
- Shower gifts.
- For letters of condolence.
- After being a guest of honor at a party.
- After a dinner at your boss's home.

Here are some situations that a thank-you note may not be expected but will come as a welcomed surprise:

- After a dinner party.
- A new acquaintance who has entertained you.
- After receiving congratulations for a birthday or graduation.
- When you receive money.
- After a job interview.

It's also handy to keep some cards with prestamped envelopes in places that are readily accessible, like your handbag or the glove compartment in your car. Then you never have an excuse not to write a thank-you note.

Sample Notes:

After receiving money:

Dear Nana,
    Thank you for the money that you sent me for my birthday. I intend to use it toward my trip to Lake Tahoe for winter break. I can't wait for the ski holiday—the mountain just had eight inches of snow. Expect a postcard in the weeks ahead.
Love,
Richard

After a job interview:

Dear Ms. Shin:

I very much appreciated your taking the time to meet with me today to explain the opening in Tailor & Trask as a copywriter.

I felt confident after our meeting that my experience suits the position you have available, particularly since I have been writing computer copy for the past two years at Flagate Software. I do hope that you will have a chance to review the sample pieces I left with you, especially the newer ones, which reflect the new Website descriptions we discussed.

I thank you for your consideration and look forward to hearing from you.

Sincerely,

Al Listfield

Stationery

Personalized stationery is not necessary, but don't use torn pieces of yellow office paper even if it is a quick note to a friend. Stroll through any card shop and you're certain to find a suitable card or notepaper for any occasion.

Invitations

The function of an invitation is to effectively give notice of an event, which, in turn, will help with the planning. I usually make a call two weeks in advance of the occasion so the person I invite can secure the date. Invitees should receive your invitation no later than one week before the event.

From e-vites to custom-designed gift baskets, invitations don't just arrive in envelopes anymore. When I hosted a lunch for my nephew's wedding, I designed the invitation on the computer. Since the affair was casual, the design was a refreshing change from all of the formal invitations many of the guests were used to receiving.

Wedding Invitations

Most wedding invitations include a reply card that should be responded to at your earliest convenience. However the old-fashioned method was reply card–deficient, and it is proper manners for the invitee to RSVP on their personal stationary.

RSVPs

I was recently asked if you can be mad if someone does not RSVP to an invitation. If an act of disrespect is enough to make you mad, then it is most certainly a valid reaction. This act is viewed as a personal affront to Paul Lerner, a publicist with London Misher Public Relations. "People should RSVP regardless of yes or no," vents Lerner. "A no is almost as important, because in organizing a party or event, it is essential to know how many people will attend, which results in the planning of the menu, the reconfiguration of the room, seating etc." If you don't hear a response by the specified time, it is appropriate for the sender to follow up with a phone call. It is possible the invitation was lost or mistakenly thrown away.

A guest should also always follow the invitation's instructions in regards to attire, arrival, departure, etc. Adds Lerner, "If the invitation admits you and one guest, don't abuse it and ask to be allowed two guests."

Letters of Complaint

If you're dissatisfied with any service or treatment, put it in writing. For a letter of complaint to be successful, your agenda should be to ultimately get results. To vent every minor disruption that your state, local cab service, or dry cleaners has caused you is an exercise in futility. However, if you do feel that you are in the right and want to be compensated, the letter should be straightforward—stick to your story, keep to the facts without transgressing to irrelevant information, and, most importantly, be polite. A letter that is antagonistic in tone may not receive the attention it deserves. Just think of saying these words face-to-face and the reaction you would receive.

The following are letters that I wrote outlining my frustrations with various service providers:

My address
Date

Contact name
Contact address

Dear Owner/Manager:

I would like to offer my comments and suggestions for my recent stay at your spa. Firstly, when my friend and I checked in, we were given a room on the golf course level where we had specifically requested *not* to be. The room had virtually no furnishings and was newly painted. After requesting for a new room with the front desk, we were eventually given a room on the second floor that overlooked the parking lot. Shortly after, my friend went to the locker room and was informed that there were no available lockers, which were filled due to day clients. They were also low on clothes (T-shirts and shorts), and often bathrobes were not available. In my opinion this is a disservice to the registered spa guests who pay more for added benefits. Registered guests should be assured the privileges that are guaranteed them, distinguished either by ID or color-coding, over daily guests.

Additionally, the shower facilities in the locker room were not clean, as expressed by other guests, and there were not enough chairs or places to sit when waiting for a treatment.

As you are aware I have been a devoted fan of your spa, coming here for almost eleven years, but I am currently dissatisfied in what I am seeing. I hope you can implement some changes, because, if the spa continues to operate as it does now, I will be left no choice but to go elsewhere.

Sincerely,

Charlotte Ford

The following letter was written to a local plumber denying his request for an inappropriate reimbursement:

My address
Date

Contact name
Contact address

Dear Contact:

I received the bill you sent me for reimbursement of your eyeglasses that fell into the cesspool while you were making an inspection at my home in Southampton.

I must say that I was quite surprised by the expenses on the bill. I feel terrible that you suffered this loss; however, I think that replacement of your glasses is your responsibility. This is an unfortunate circumstance, but one that is personal in nature.

You have done a great deal of work in my home, and I hope we can continue to have a good working relationship.

Sincerely,

Charlotte Ford

The following is a letter I wrote in regards to dissatisfaction in attending a fund-raiser that misrepresented the event:

My address
Date

Contact name
Contact address

Dear Contact:

    I recently attended a luncheon honoring [the wife of a presidential candidate] at the home of [name omitted] here in New York. Quite frankly these types of affairs generally do not interest me, but, being told that it would be an intimate affair and that if I RSVP'd promptly, I would be assured a "very good seat," I accepted immediately. I do not have any political affiliation, but was interested to hear what [the candidate's wife] had to say about the campaign. When I arrived and heard that there were 100 guests expected and it would not be a seated lunch, I was a bit miffed. I was led to believe that my donation of $1,000 afforded me the opportunity to attend an exclusive gathering where I would be able to converse with [the candidate's wife].

    I now feel it important to express my concern because I am sure that [candidate's wife] would be interested in knowing and, most certainly, would not want to mislead other potential supporters of her husband's campaign. It's still early enough in the campaign to avoid any similar mishaps.

    I would be most grateful for a response at your earliest convenience.

Sincerely,

Charlotte Ford

Holiday Cards

I send almost 500 holiday cards every season. Whether sent to old friends or to a new professional contact, cards keep relations alive. Similar to invitations, it is always best to make the extra effort to personalize your card. A truly unique card will stand out among all of the Hallmark look-alikes. A tradition in my family is to send a family portrait—the image says more than words. Some people like to include letters that update distant friends and family or personal events that occurred during the year.

Letters of a Personal Nature

Occasionally heavy emotions, whether of a romantic or despondent nature, are best expressed in letter form. For those who find it difficult to communicate their feelings, a letter can provide a therapeutic release. When written with care, one's true sentiments can be aptly expressed. They can also be read over and saved by the receiver.

Condolence Letters

Believe it or not, the key to writing a good condolence letter is not eloquence. In fact, it may not even be noticed. A good letter mustn't seem as if it was taken straight from an etiquette book. It is more important that the letter includes words of sincerity, comfort, and something personal. A specific remembrance of the deceased—perhaps an account of specific qualities or events—can offer deeper consolation than any clever line or turn of a phrase. Add concrete comfort by offering your services. This could be in the form of an invitation for a weekend or assistance in any household errands, in which case you must follow up with a definite invitation for the near future.

Most commercial sympathy cards are, I think, commercial. If you must send one, it's wise to include your own note. After my mother's passing, some of the warmest letters were expressed in just a few sentences. In fact, I've saved these letters, which have assisted me when writing my own. Following are some samples that may help you.

To someone who lost a parent:

Dear Mr. Kimbell:

Please accept my sincerest sympathy at this time. I know that the loss of your mother is a difficult one, as she was very close to you, and many others. She was a very fine woman and my prayers are with you and your family.

Dear Robert:

The death of a parent is always more profound than one can know in advance. It is without a doubt the saddest event of one's life and certainly leaves a void that can never be completely filled.

My own mother's death left me so bereft. The one whom I loved to make proud could show her pride no longer. In the meantime, in the optimism of our faith, we can look forward to another life in the future together in joyful reunion with those who have given life to us in the present.

Dear Allison:

I am so sorry about your mother's passing. We become parents ourselves long before we stop being children. My thoughts and prayers are with you.

To a family friend:

Dear Mrs. Cooper:

I was saddened to hear of Jason's death. Although I haven't seen Jason in a long while, I thought of him often with a deep affection. My sympathy and dearest love are with you during this difficult time.

To an acquaintance:

Dear Edward:

It was with great sadness to hear of Samantha's death. I shall remember her always as a wonderful lady who graced our world. It is said that the best respect you can pay someone is to take one of her traits and make it your own. I shall strive to be more of a lady as she was.

Replies to Condolence Letters

Your reply can be brief, and it need not be written immediately upon receiving the condolence letter. If you receive hundreds of letters, it is to those you know only slightly, appropriate to send a printed card (either on heavy bond white paper or traditional mourning paper with a black border).

Past Century/ Present Century
Social correspondence was once considered the women's domain, while the men were mentioned in the body of the letter. Now that men and women have shared household responsibilities, both parties address letters.

You may wish to reply personally on the card. After my parents died, I wrote hundreds of letters that took months to complete. Printed cards were sent to hundreds of others who sent flowers and cards.

A printed card might read:

The family of Ms. (or Mrs.) Sandra Curtis deeply appreciates (or thanks you for) your thoughtfulness.

DO'S

1. Do send a business letter on company stationery or personal letterhead.
2. Do get straight to the point when writing a letter.
3. Do refer to a professional contact by her first name if you know her socially.
4. Do be polite when writing a letter of complaint.
5. Do send Christmas cards as a way to keep in touch with old friends.

DON'TS

1. Don't send a letter without making certain that it is grammatically correct.

② Don't feel it necessary that a personal letter be sent on per-
    sonal stationery.

③ Don't feel obliged to send a reply to a condolence letter
    immediately after you receive it.

④ Don't consider family correspondence to be assigned exclu-
    sively to the lady of the house.

CORRESPONDENCE QUIZ

A business letter must contain:
- A.   The date.
- B.   The business's address.
- C.   Your contact information.
- D.   All of the above.

ANSWER: D

"Miss" should not be used for:
- A.   A woman who is dating someone.
- B.   A young lady with intentions of getting married.
- C.   An older lady.
- D.   A professional woman.

ANSWER: C

The correct way to address a married woman is:
- A.   "Mrs. John Winston."
- B.   "Ms. Lucy Winston."
- C.   By her maiden name.
- D.   All of the above.

ANSWER: D

It is mandatory to send a thank-you note after:
- A.   A job interview.
- B.   Being a weekend guest with friends.
- C.   When you receive money.
- D.   After receiving congratulations from a birthday or graduation.

ANSWER: B

An invitation may be sent:
- A. Up to the day of the event as long as you call first.
- B. The week of the event.
- C. At least two weeks before the event.
- D. None of the above.

ANSWER: C

You should RSVP:
- A. Only if you can't attend.
- B. It's not necessary to RSVP.
- C. If you want to add another guest.
- D. Regardless if it's yes or no.

ANSWER: D

Expert Advice

Helen Gurley Brown, Editor in Chief of *Cosmopolitan* international editions, Author of *The Writer's Rules,* and Devoted Correspondent

Put It in Writing

Helen Gurley Brown began her career as a secretary in an advertising agency. Impressing her boss, Don Belding, with her original and entertaining letters, she eventually became a copywriter in his agency and went on to become one of the nation's highest-paid advertising copywriters.

In 1962, Helen Brown wrote the best-seller Sex and the Single Girl, *which was also made into a movie starring Natalie Wood and Tony Curtis. She has since written* Sex and the Office—*also a best-seller,* The Outrageous Opinions of Helen Gurley Brown, Helen Gurley Brown's Single Girl's Cookbook, *and* Sex and the New Single Girl, *an updated version of her original book.*

In 1965, Helen Brown became editor in chief of Cosmopolitan, *and the result is publishing history. Since that time, the magazine's sales and advertising have risen spectacularly.* Cosmo *now sells just under 3 million copies and is one of the five largest-selling magazines in the United States.*

Her book, Having It All *(ten years in the writing), was published in the fall of 1982 and remained on the* New York Times *Best-seller List for four months. The paperback edition was also a best-seller.* The Late Show: A Semiwild but Practical Survival Plan for Women Over 50, *was published in 1993, and in 1998 Helen introduced* The Writer's Rules, The Power of Positive Prose—How to Create It and Get It Published. *Her newest book,* I'm Wild Again: Snippets from My Life and a Few Brazen Thoughts, *was published in February 2000.*

Writing a note is an act of philanthropy. There isn't anyone who doesn't fish though the junk mail for that personal letter. Luckily, between my husband and me, there is always a note in the mailbox from someone—one of the bonuses of sending so much personal mail. A passionate letter writer and receiver, I am better a writer than talker!

So, how to write those notes with flair?

- Start with a question, like "Are you the best friend or what?"
- Keep them short. As interesting as little Bobby's scoring the winning goal is to you, it may not hold the interest of your recipient.
- Pace yourself. If a word doesn't need to be in the sentence, take it out.
- If you're writing a letter of anger, wait awhile, maybe even a few days, before you send it. Like an argument, it's always a wise idea to simmer your anger before reacting through words.
- It's all in the details. If you received a gift from someone, tell him or her about the fabulous angel food cake you created with the new mixer or how useful the extra cash was on your trip to Guadeloupe.

There's a lot of talk about e-mail eliminating the handwritten letter the way Starbucks is squeezing out the little cafés. I happen to love those little cafés with their special blends and quirky decor. Sure, gossiping is fun on e-mail—who doesn't banter back and forth about latest movies or sitcoms? But those exchanges happen in a flash. They don't have the charm or staying power the way a personal note does.

My mother saved all of my letters. I took them back and I have yet to read them. I intend to on a rainy day. I keep all of my personal letters—I have a big Liz Smith file and I believe she has a file of mine.

Like fine wine and vintage couture, a letter's value will only increase—write and save. So nice to correspond with you!

CHAPTER VIII

SINGLE PROCESS

*L*unches are shorter, days are longer, glass ceilings are great for adding extra light, and dating is no longer the way it was back when Mom and Dad *courted,* thanks in part to the working woman. Just look at television's most popular shows in recent history. It seems Father is no longer the only one who knows best. The eighties had such hits as *Family Ties* and *The Cosby Show.* The nineties were spent with *Friends.* The twenty-first century celebrates *Sex and the City* and *Ally McBeal.* Notice a trend? Today's programming is moving away from family to independent, single characters—many of them focusing on the independent female. This current pattern throws some new guidelines into the relationship mix. A man can no longer assume financial superiority to a woman who is successful in her own right. But should she still expect the man to be the sole supplier? How can two working people plan a date when professional life trumps personal life? Once meeting Mr. or Ms. Right was as simple as having an attraction and sharing a few interests. Today, on-the-go single people are dealing with a whole new set of possibilities and rules.

No Time to Date

If your day begins regularly at 9:00 A.M. and ends at 5:00 P.M., you should probably count your blessings. For most of us, the workday has limitless parameters. Lunch is a quick sandwich hastily shoveled down in between meetings, and by the end of the day you may be so fried that the only energy you may have is to call for takeout. So who has time to date? Like a business meeting or doctor's appointment, dating for many has become an obligation. However, when life takes its cue from the office, consider your priorities. If you have a genuine desire to date, you'll find that you can make the time.

If you are open to meeting people, others will sense that. You can always pick up on someone's interest by honing in on buzzwords or subtle come-ons such as "Are you here with anyone?" or "We have so much in common."

Changing your single status is like getting a new job—if you want something, you have to go after it. Sometimes a relationship needs a little push, some extra effort, unless you're considering online dating (which I

don't recommend). A good way to meet other people is through friends. Start aligning yourself with a clique that has a lot of other single friends. If the relationship does work out, you'll never have to argue with your mate over whose group of friends you want to go out with.

What About *The Book of Rules*?

The Dating Game was a gimmicky television show on which sun-kissed Californians asked one another pointless questions and competed for the raciest answer in order to secure a date. *The Dating Game* is not what you do in order to secure a stable relationship built on honesty—an old-fashioned value that will always endure. For those who premeditate on how many days you should respond to a phone call—or accept a date depending on when you were asked out—that's a game. A relationship's most exhilarating period is often in its beginning stages, when you're dizzied by the prospects of seeing your prospective other and you don't want the night to end. It's learning about that person early on in the dating process that's most exciting, so why spoil the sensation by following a set of guidelines?

While some may argue that a little aloofness can intensify the desire, there's a difference between some savvy calculation and intentional deceit.

Asking Someone Out

If you are attracted to someone, and would like to ask her out, e-mail is a great way to break the ice. The message could simply read: "I really enjoyed meeting you. Would you like to go out for a drink sometime?" This gives the person a fair amount of time to consider the invitation without being caught off guard. If the invitation is accepted, a phone call is then in order to set the date.

Drinks at a bar is a common way to spend a first date. With drinks, you are not committed to an entire evening. If drinks go well, you could always go onwards and upwards, and have a dinner together.

Declining an unwanted invitation is difficult. You must be tactful yet firm. One all-purpose and final way out of a date is to say, "Thank you, but this is not a good time for me right now."

A woman asking a man out

She earns a comparable living, she's independent and self-assured. Today's woman no longer has to wait to be asked out. It's also a relief for all sexes not to follow such a strict set of rules. Scott Dynan, a young investment banker, says simply, "It takes the pressure off of me."

If you do want to ask a man out, a good way to do so is to have a plan in mind—tickets to an event, a party, skating in the park. This kind of date is more low-key than something more intimate.

Guess Who's Paying for Dinner

Waiters had it easier when the man was the provider—the one who would always pick up the check at dinner. Now that a woman earns her own income, sometimes making as much as her dinner companion, how can she expect to be wined and dined yet still assert her newfound financial independence?

"It wouldn't even occur to me to have a woman ever pay the bill," says James Morrow, a magazine writer, on dating women.

"When the check came, he asked me for my share. I was appalled," says Joanne Napolitano, a television producer, about a date she had where the man asked her out. "Even if his intentions were friendly rather than romantic, it's only polite for him to take care of the bill. I would have been more than happy to pay for the second dinner," she adds.

Okay, so what's the standard? The early stages of dating are awkward as it is without the added pressure of the arrival of the dinner bill. But don't sell this moment short. It's an event that can often make or break a burgeoning relationship. Thus there should be a few simple rules to follow. Take note:

1. Who Asked Whom?

He Asked Her

If the man asked the woman out, he should pay.

"He should cover the check, but she should still offer," suggests James Morrow. "Otherwise she may appear too willing, somewhat selfish." The woman could smoothly handle the arrival of the bill by saying, in her most sincere tone, "Can I help with that?" This is also an opportunity for the man to establish guidelines for the future. For instance, he may say, "You can get it the next time."

What she should not do once the bill arrives is appear to have her hands tied behind her back or suddenly excuse herself from the table.

She Asked Him

If the woman asked the man, it would be presumptuous for her to expect him to pay. What a coup—just ask every unattached male out on a date and expect a free meal. If it's a mutually agreeable date, and he offers, she should kindly protest. If he makes a counteroffer, reaching for his wallet with genuine insistence, obliging his chivalrous gesture is just—chivalrous.

The Man Who Always Insists on Paying

If it becomes a comfortable routine that your new male companion always attends to the expenses, let's face it, ladies, he's worth having! But, in all true respects, a woman should feel obliged to reciprocate. This gesture doesn't necessarily have to be paid back by a dinner invitation—tickets to the opera, preparing him dinner, or even a thoughtful gift, such as a book that she recommended to him. If she does make a special invitation to take him to dinner, she should begin the evening by simply saying, "It's on me."

2. After the Second Date

If you made it into the third or fourth dinner date, as enjoyable as eating out can be, realistically, it's also costly. The woman should offer to pay for the bill, especially if it is at a restaurant she chose. A savvy response from the male would be, "I have it covered, why don't you pay for cocktails" (or ice cream, the movie, or the cab ride home). He could also add, "Next time we can go dutch." By the fifth or sixth date, you have a better gauge of that person you are involved with.

Brokering the Blind Date

You may have two friends you're dying to fix up together on a blind date. There are several ways to accomplish this, but first it's important that both parties agree to the date. Once this is established, you may:

1. Have the two parties accompany you and your companion to a dinner, or another event.
2. Give the man your friend's number so he can ask her out.

After the friends have met, it's up to them to decide whether or not they want to continue seeing each other. If you receive calls from both parties and one is interested whereas the other is not, try not to get too involved. It's now up to them to figure it out, and it's unfair for anyone to place you in the middle.

Dating in the Workplace

Although we've established that no one seems to have any time to date, there is still a stronger likelihood of meeting someone where the majority of your time is spent—the office. Once considered taboo, the office romance was a discreet affair only exposed if the relationship was discovered, resulted in marriage, or if someone left the company to take another job. Now dating in the office is commonplace. However, rules of decorum still apply.

Ilene Rosenzweig, editor of The New York Times "Styles" section, is involved with Rick Marin, also an employee at the Times. The policy at the

Times is that couples cannot report to one another, because of concern about getting or giving preferential treatment. However, dating is allowed, and according to Rosenzweig, there can be many benefits to such a situation. "What I experience," says Rosenzweig, "is the added value of someone who really understands the situation because they *know* you. You don't have to catch up telegraphically—you understand the context. It really depends on your relationship. For instance, I really value being able to speak directly with Rick and, of course, there's always lunch." She further adds that the professional distance is good for the relationship. "When Rick and I leave the office, suddenly we can be together—it's exiting, almost elicit. There's a suppressed flirtation." Following are some considerations Rosenzweig recommends:

- Be mindful of any special attention, private exchanges, or other personal gestures.
- Couples need to be mindful not to lapse into the kind of comfortable rapport that they have outside the office—meaning no P.D.A. (Public Display of Affection).
- If you're having a fight, you must remove yourself from the issues in the office. This is what Rosenzweig refers to as "not bringing the old storm cloud to the office." Find a quick resolution and be careful not to antagonize the situation based on the fight.
- "Don't go to work together! Probably 90 percent of our arguments result from waiting for the other person—the same goes for leaving."
- And just because you work together, that's no excuse not to be romantic. "Yes, you can send flowers, even if they're just two desks away," adds Rosenzweig.

Dating During a Divorce

Divorce can be a difficult and confusing time. Finding happiness in someone else's company may seem enticing. This can, however, pose legal as well as social problems. As important as it is to meet other people and establish a new life for yourself, if papers have yet to be signed, you'd better ask your lawyer to explain the divorce laws and how they apply to your situation.

Since you're paying a divorce lawyer a good deal for his advice, take it. If you would like to see someone during your divorce but your lawyer is against it, it's best to be honest with the prospective date and let him or her know just that.

If you are out with someone and unexpectedly meet friends who are not aware of your circumstances, don't evade the situation. Before everyone's minds go into spin cycle, make your introductions and add that the person you're with is a friend. If your simple statement will not suffice, say, "I'm currently in the middle of a divorce," or "Max and I are getting a divorce."

Suddenly Unattached

Just as hard as it is to date, some may find it even harder to be newly single. Your usually busy Friday night suddenly becomes free. Weekly groceries are now bought for one. You may need some time with this new lifestyle and to reacquaint yourself with that once-single person—you!

After getting over the stigma of being a "single" opposed to a "couple," you have shown yourself how comfortable you are on your own. But don't be surprised by the friends who want to change your status. It's really up to you when you are ready to begin dating. Most newly single people go along with the fix-ups for the first few times, though even the most outgoing refuse such invitations after a while—a string of bad blind dates can swear the most relationship ambitious person off of dating entirely. Usually the situation is contrived, making all parties uncomfortable. It's always better to meet people where you feel most natural. And they will most likely have a better chance of getting to know your more genuine side.

Older Men, Younger Women

The next time you see a male acquaintance at a restaurant with a significantly younger woman, never say, "Is this your daughter?" There is always a strong possibility that this woman is his significant other. As established dating has become more liberal, it is no longer biased by age or any other constraints. In order for a relationship between an older man and younger woman to work, the man may have to indulge in her desire to go snowboarding for the weekend whereas she may need to endure a few opera concerts.

A man may encounter severe criticism from friends, especially if he divorced his wife and she is still part of their social circle. Instead of abandoning your old friends entirely, have them meet your new girlfriend so they can understand why she makes you happy. In regards to her meeting your children, you cannot force them to accept her (see Chapter XII "Etiquette During Life's Challenges"). It may be a hard adjustment and take longer than you had hoped, but if the relationship is meant to be, everyone should come around.

Likewise, if the relationship does become serious, telling her parents may be difficult, especially if the new boyfriend has a few years on daddy. The woman should speak to her parents with sensitivity to their obvious concerns. It's also sensible for everyone to spend an evening together, possibly at the couple's favorite restaurant so they are in surroundings in which they feel comfortable. Hopefully, when her parents see how happy and natural the couple is with each other, they will soften up and become more accepting of the idea.

Older Women, Younger Men

Cher and Madonna do it—revel in the romance of younger men, that is. It's long been accepted for a woman to openly date a younger man. However, these couples do face some particular challenges.

Since the woman is older, she's likely to be more established in her career. A younger man just starting out is therefore likely to earn less money than she. If so, a woman has a few options: She may pay his way, or she may change her lifestyle so that it is more in line with his.

At the time a forty-year-old friend of mine fell in love with a twenty-eight-year-old man, her salary far exceeded his. While she simply could have given him money from time to time, she feared he would have felt like a gigolo. Instead she chose to scale down her own lifestyle. The couple ate at affordable restaurants (always splitting the check), went to movies as opposed to the theater, and took camping trips. Always remember there will be a little give and take in any relationship.

The Single Target

Today single people have their niche in society. They must check their own box on important documents, have their own special nights at clubs, and can't attend family day at the office without feeling a little out of place. This group, however, does have rights.

Remember, single people can be unattached for a variety of reasons. Some are intentionally independent, others may have a desire to become part of a couple but haven't settled on a partner yet. Whatever the reason, the single people in your life shouldn't be treated like second-class citizens. Don't shy away from inviting your bachelor cousin Peter to your kids' birthday parties just because you think he might feel out of place as the only adult without a child. Invite him because you want to see him and he wants to see you. He would probably be more hurt if you didn't include him at all.

By the same token, a married couple shouldn't feel obliged to ask their single friend Marcy to dinner only because unattached friend Bill will also be in attendance. Ask Marcy to dinner because she tells great stories and is fun to be around. Three at a table shouldn't be awkward at all. And, remember, though there are certainly lifestyle differences that don't mesh between married couples and single people, it's no reason to dramatically adjust a relationship.

No one likes to be marked as different. The same way a person who has lost a job doesn't always want to hear "How's the job search?," a single person does not want to always be asked about her single status as if it is some kind of abnormality.

Breaking Up

To quote the cheesy song, "breaking up is hard to do." Simply said, there's no easy way to handle a breakup. It's been done in as many ways as there are reasons to separate. However, there are many breakup don'ts. First and foremost, even if you have the spine of a jellyfish, never end a relationship over the phone, by a letter, a proxy, or any other method where direct contact is not involved. It must be done in person.

Naturally, conduct the breakup as thoughtfully as possible, citing only key issues—his "shallow friends" or her "bad haircut" are facts that don't need to be made known. If there is someone else and your soon-to-be ex asks about this, be honest. You should be the one to break the news, because finding it out from another person may be more hurtful. This could also grant the closure to the relationship you both need. If you foresee an intense but necessary release of emotions, then choose a setting where you can have some privacy.

If you find a complete breakup tremendously unsettling, a dramatic departure from the life you are accustomed to, a "casual breakup" could help ease the process. Remaining friends, still having the occasional dinner together, conversing by e-mail, and engaging in a weekly catch-up call are all simple enough routines to maintain strong relations. However, this situation should be handled carefully as it could also lead one person on, giving him other false hope, which is extremely unfair, almost torturous, and can only prolong the agony for all parties.

Try to maintain a sensible approach and try to have a good handle on your true emotions. If you are meant to be, the relationship will take its destined course. I know of a woman who broke up with her boyfriend because she needed to focus on her career. She was so impressed with how he handled the breakup, however, that they eventually got back together. Though I do not encourage ending a breakup with the hope of getting back together, remaining rational can alleviate the difficulty of what is a sometimes devastating process.

Most importantly, be sensitive. There is no way of knowing how someone can handle such news. If someone you break it off with reacts by putting sugar in your car's fuel tank or disparaging your character to all of your friends, just remember, breaking up is hard to do.

Let's Be Friends

For some the words are as painful as "You're fired." For those who value the relationship but realize that it's not meant to be on an intimate level, choosing to maintain the friendship is extremely adult. Though the transition of partner to pal will undoubtedly be uncomfortable, it may be worth it in order to save a close relation. There are also some situations where a couple may have shared the same group of friends, and why should you have to avoid one another. Hopefully a brief time apart is all you need to reassess and re-approach your future together. A couple may want to meet after the healing has occurred, and you can go on with your lives without someone having to move to another district.

Getting Back Together

So the "breaker upper" would like to schedule a postmortem meeting, possibly leading to a reconciliation based on the difficult time that has resulted during the time apart. Just remember that a new haircut, that sexy outfit, and good food on the burner doesn't necessitate an instant reconciliation. A little time apart doesn't shroud the initial hurt. There are issues to get through, and this may be the only opportunity that you have to get your points conveyed. Just as an award recipient brings notes with him before making the speech, you may want to write down your issues so you are properly prepared. Here are some don'ts to keep in mind:

- Don't orchestrate your little brother or sister to call during the meeting, so that their screened message saying "how great last night was" can be openly heard. The same goes for having flowers delivered to yourself.
- Don't lie.

- Don't act like a diva or martyr.
- Don't be catty if the conversation isn't going well, and request all of the presents that you gave him back.
- Don't ever say, "I was the best thing you ever had."

My Place or Yours?

For the couple that is seriously involved, it is only natural that they spend most of their time together, usually at one of their homes. During this period, emotions and economics can influence a serious decision—the "let's live together" decision. With marriage being the eventual commitment, living with someone allows a couple to really learn about each other before they exchange vows. When the time comes to ask, not "pop" the question, it's best to open a discussion by asking simply, "How do you feel about living together?"

When living together, the "What movie should we rent?" debacle becomes an amateur discussion compared with who made what phone call, who left the milk out on the counter, and who gets the bigger closet space. (The larger closet space should be given to the one who has a larger wardrobe.) It's safe to assume that many of the issues that occupy a married couple will plague couples that live together as well. Don't toss in the towel every time it gets a bit difficult.

Keep in mind, however, it's best to not share a home with someone out of the sake of convenience or financial advantages or, for that matter, with a relatively new flame. Since relations and personal space are intertwined, not to mention finances, the scenario is not as simple as it may seem.

Giving the news to the family

Different families will react differently to the news "We're moving in together." Keep in mind, the previous generation usually got married before living together. Your significant other's parents may take the news with the enthusiasm expected from an engagement announcement while your family may view your relation as the moral corrupter.

It's not fair to be overly judgmental of how your or your relation's parents handle the news. Some families may be disturbed for social or religious reasons by a couple's living together; others tend to see marriage for their child as a sign that he or she is settling down. In other words, the emotional and financial responsibility for that child is no longer their primary concern.

When approaching family with the news, be sensitive. Hopefully your family has met the new girlfriend or boyfriend and understands the nature of the relationship. Be open with your family. Discuss all of the reasons that have led you both to this decision—from not being ready to making a full commitment to expecting to marry in the near future. Above all, be honest. Your family will be more likely to feel that you are acting in an adult and responsible manner.

When You Don't Approve of Your Friend's Relationship

It happens to us all, your close friend is dating someone you don't feel is right for her. As tempting as it may be, don't share your views. Even if this is the friend you spent the third grade with, had your first beer with, and made the pledge that you'd be friends till the end with—when it comes to friends and romance, it can only get you into trouble, so, zip it. Even during those moments when she wants to vent her frustrations about her relationship, don't espouse your negative views. Once they patch things up, she'll still remember.

DO'S

1. Do make the effort if you have a genuine desire to date.
2. Do offer to help pay when the bill arrives.
3. Do introduce friends to your younger girlfriend.
4. Do remain friends with a former boyfriend or girlfriend if you feel you're able.

5 Do seriously consider the advantages of living with someone.

DON'TS

1. Don't play games in order to secure an honest relationship.
2. Don't treat single friends differently just because you are in a relationship.
3. Don't feel that you have to go on blind dates just because you are newly single.
4. Don't go into unnecessary details when breaking up with someone.

SINGLE PROCESS QUIZ

If a man asks a woman out:
    A.   He should pay for the evening.
    B.   They should go Dutch.
    C.   He should pay for the dinner and she should offer to pay for dessert, cab ride, movie, or other nominal expense of the evening.
    D.   Any of the above.
ANSWER: A

If a woman asks a man out:
    A.   He can pay.
    B.   She should pay.
    C.   They should go Dutch.
    D.   Any of the above.
ANSWER: D

If you're in the middle of a divorce, you should:
    A.   Date excessively to establish your new life.
    B.   Check with your soon-to-be ex-spouse first.
    C.   Ask your lawyer if it is legally permissible to date.
    D.   Wait until the divorce papers are signed.
ANSWER: C

A woman who is dating a significantly older man should tell her parents:
    A.   Only when it is serious.
    B.   With sensitivity to their obvious concerns.
    C.   Confidently.
    D.   When her boyfriend asks to meet them.
ANSWER: B

Break up:

    A. Over the phone.

    B. By letter.

    C. Through a friend.

    D. None of the above.

ANSWER: D

You shouldn't live with a significant other:

    A. Because you are considering getting married.

    B. If you want to take the relationship further.

    C. For the sake of convenience.

    D. All of the above.

ANSWER: C

IN LIVING MATRIMONY

*W*hat's great about marriage is having that one person with whom you can *share* your life. Sharing: an altruistic concept that is as sweet and generous as your granny's candy dish. But, for some, the concept of sharing living space can be as distasteful as that squirt of licorice you so dislike unexpectedly oozing from a cherry–flavored candy shell. A good marriage is based on many things. Some hold communication and love as the key to success, while others place respect and devotion at the top of the list. No matter what, every relationship involves a grown–up version of sharing. In regards to etiquette (as I am not a marriage counselor), consideration to your spouse is the most challenging rule in the book. Manners can often be overlooked when it comes to dealing with the one who knows you best. However, this is exactly where manners are most important. I say: Show the person you love respect and courtesy. What marriage counselor could argue that?

The Prenup

The prenuptial contract always seems to make for good tabloid material. In real life, there is certain to be some drama once the prenup is presented.

143

The recipient may initially interpret it as the fiancé having doubts on the future of the marriage. However, according to divorce lawyer Raul Felder, these days the prenup is as standard as a marriage license.

For those sentimentalists out there, try to approach the document with a practical understanding. Felder rationalizes that the prenup has nothing to do with romance. "One shouldn't allow it to get beyond that point, it's a document to protect everyone." According to Felder, divorce laws are more intrusive and expensive, so a prenuptial agreement will prevent such hardships that could prove later to be emotionally and financially devastating. A variety of prenuptials can be drafted—such as ones that are nullified after a certain number of years, accumulated wealth, etc.

When presenting the agreement to your betrothed, tact and manners are key—this is why Felder advises your lawyer to handle the dirty work. Again, such legalese should have nothing to do with romance and should never infringe upon your life as a couple.

Sharing

"Time to share!" Remember when you had to share everything with your brother or sister? Those hard-learned lessons will now come in handy. It's time to graduate to sharing's next level. Though you're no longer talking about sharing turns on the Big Wheel, marriage is still a constant exercise in sharing. This can be as simple as sharing a medicine cabinet, the remote control, or the toss-up on who gets the right side of the bed. However generous the "What's mine is yours" ethic may be, the reality of finding only a drop of milk for your morning cereal makes all warm sentiments easy to forget. You'll need to develop systems you both can abide by. He gets the top shelf, she the bottom. Mondays he watches the game and Thursdays she can watch *Friends*. To avoid any relapses into the single life, some planning, compassion, and consideration could make the adjustment easier. And, if you use the last of the milk, at least have the courtesy to go to the store and replace it, or alert your spouse.

Decorating Together

My philosophy when it comes to decorating is that the men should stay out of it! All right, this contradicts the idea of sharing. If you decide to attempt shared decorating, just be prepared for a lot of compromise. If he prefers modern retro and she likes country traditional, look for ways to blend both tastes.

From selecting the bath towels to the dining room table, decorating is costly enough to make it a slow process. You have time to make decisions opposed to buying instantly, and my advice is to take it. Since buying a couch is not like buying a sweater (it's more expensive and will probably last much longer), it won't hurt to sit on throw pillows while you shop around for something you both love. Married life is based on building a future. Just as you've invested in another person, take care to create a substantive home.

Redecorating with a Spouse Who Was Previously Married

If your new spouse will be moving into the house that you shared with your former spouse, redecorating to some extent is essential. Otherwise, you may feel that you aren't sharing a household so much as entertaining a permanent guest, a permanent guest who feels awkward and uncomfortable among everyday reminders of a former partner.

If there are new stepchildren who will also be moving in, their feelings and needs are a major consideration. They may be attached to some of the pieces of furniture from their former home. Thus, when beginning the new decorating, you should involve the children, making them feel that this really is their new home. Allow them to participate, especially in decorating their new rooms. It's important for them to feel they have a place of their own in this new life.

If the children won't be living with you full-time, they should still be apprised on the changes that you are making so they can mentally prepare for a new home, rather than be overwhelmed when entering a dramatically different place for the first time. If the room that they stay in is also the guest room, allow them to add their own decorations. The anonymity of a guest room can make a child feel more like a visitor than a member of the family.

Every member of this new family will have their quirks. The children may be accustomed to having a television set in the kitchen to watch the morning shows whereas you may appreciate the formality of eating in the dining room. It won't do to enforce your will by shifting meals into the dining room. Instead, ask your new family to indulge your whim and eat in the dining room occasionally.

Sharing Closets

For couples who have different organizational habits or simply too much stuff, sharing closet space is a quarrel waiting to happen. If there's only one closet in the bedroom, then you may consider special shelving. Otherwise try assigning one of you another closet in the house, even if it's in an inconvenient location. Another option would be to stow items that are not as frequently worn in the second closet to at least create some more space. The closet outside the bedroom could be designated to whoever gets up earlier so that the one still sleeping is not disturbed. It stands to reason that the person with the larger wardrobe should get the bigger closet. Once again, sharing closets comes back to working things out together. It's also a great forum to hone your skills in problem solving.

Sharing a Bathroom

Who hasn't experienced the infuriating morning lockout episode? You woke up late for work or school, you stumble to the bathroom door only to find it locked from the inside with your brother, roommate, or visiting Uncle Jack singing happily away in the shower. In a marriage, the morning routine is something that must be worked out early on.

Naturally the person who leaves earlier should shower earlier—and, unless you don't mind being secretly disparaged, always leave enough hot water for the other person. Another idea is to shower at the gym if you happen to work out in the morning.

If undue abuse of your personal belongings occurs—characterized by a loofah that's shredded to bits or a razor that feels dull as a butter knife—designate the shelf space in your medicine cabinet into "His" and "Hers" sections. It's all about the nature of a relationship, a little compromise and consideration.

Also, keep in mind of gender specific peeves. For example:

FOR HIM: "Put the toilet seat down!" is not just a mantra women created to annoy you. Imagine if you got up to use the bathroom in the middle of the night only to sit on a seatless toilet and fall into the basin. You'd be pretty angry, I'll bet.

FOR HER: Leaving tampon wrappers, makeup-stained cotton balls, and other feminine items lying around is not only gross to look at, it's dirty. Make the added effort to toss such things away as opposed to reinforcing to your spouse's belief that women really are impossible to understand.

Sharing a Bed

The idea of sharing the same bed with someone, cuddling throughout the night, is not as romantic and cozy as it may seem. Many new couples may discover that they can barely sleep through the night, exhausted by the blanket tugs-of-war, being edged to the side of the bed while the spouse is in a spread-eagle position, or enduring a snore as loud as a diesel engine. Rather than hitting the hay each evening fraught with anxiety that it will be an all-night battle, your rest and health depends on you discussing the problem with your partner. Chances are your spouse may be experiencing the same turmoil. Simply say, "I love the idea that we can spend the night together in one bed, but I can't seem to be able to sleep." And then reach a solution together.

Sex aficionados may deem a king-size bed as the inspiration behind a king-size sex life. I think those sleepless couples worn out by continual struggles over territory inspired the larger beds. The larger the bed, the better chance a couple has at having a good night's sleep. I know of one couple intent on making their sleep time successful by simply equipping the bed with two of everything—two blankets, two sets of sheets, etc. The only drawback is that it makes for interesting bed dressing.

For those who have tried but are unable to sleep together in the same bed, the simplest solution is to buy two twin beds with separate linens and push them together with one blanket on top. When it comes time to sleep, just add another blanket.

Sharing Finances

With marriage, not only do you gain a new husband, family, and lifestyle, but, for some people, a joint checking account is also a splendid bonus. Financial sharing, however, is an aspect of marriage that should be approached with extreme caution, as finances are the result of many household arguments and can cause couples to separate. This is another situation where an open discussion and rules need to be implemented at the outset. If you anticipate turmoil in this area, one easy option is to have separate accounts. According to Harvey I. Sladkus, Esq., American and International Academies of Matrimonial Lawyers in *Bottom Line-Personal,* he advises married couples to maintain separate holdings rather than commingle them in one account. "Each spouse can keep any assets acquired before marriage or ones obtained through gifts or inheritance (even after marriage) in his/her own account so long as the non-titled spouse does not contribute to the increase in value of the other spouse's separate property. This makes the source of funds clear."

Each household must follow its own rules, with regard to family money, inheritance, and retirement. Couples need to work out the allocation of funds carefully and responsibly. Following are a few generic scenarios:

The spouse who doesn't work

For the wife or husband who stays home, attending to all domestic needs, he or she should have an allowance. If you're newly married, a sensible method in figuring out a rate is to spend a month recording your regular expenses, then determine a figure based on this amount.

The professional couple

Again, the division of funds should be worked out between the couple early on, preferably before the wedding day, to avoid any catastrophic outcomes. Funds and expenses could be divided. Or the one with the higher income could spend more on domestic expenses.

He earns more

If the husband has the higher income level, he could take care of the bigger expenses, such as the mortgage, insurance, etc. She could buy her own clothes and personal items. Household bills could be divided among the couple, or set up a joint account strictly for all domestic expenses.

She earns more

She could pay the bulk of expenses, but whenever fair and reasonable, he should contribute. The couple may also consider having an additional allowance for the husband.

Different Sets of Friends

How convenient it would be if you and your spouse met through a mutual set of friends, inheriting the same social stratosphere that you enjoyed before marriage. If this is not the case, couples have most likely met each other's friends and will soon realize that some friends will work seamlessly into their life as a married couple while others will be cause for more compromise. If your spouse doesn't particularly get along with some of your friends, try to maintain a relationship with those friends without your spouse's involvement. If the friend is extremely dear, ask your spouse to make an effort every once in a while. When it comes to socializing with business acquaintances, an effort must be made. Unless he's expecting you to socialize with business acquaintances on a regular basis, for the few times you might have to get together, it shouldn't be a big deal, it's just a little effort.

The In-laws

If you naturally get along with the in-laws, great; you should conduct seminars and educate the rest of us on how it's done.

When your in-laws prove difficult to get along with, you should still make the effort—it made life so much easier for me. Keep in mind that though your in-laws are gaining a child, in a sense they are also losing one. Respect for your in-laws is a custom that should always be upheld—it's an unspoken courtesy. Allowing a few issues to slip a little will be easier for everyone.

If there are in-law disagreements that occur frequently, and they're causing a strain on your marriage or your sanity, you can address them, oh so politely: "Can you just hear me out? You may not agree, but . . ."

Holidays

When holidays, vacations, and celebrations roll around, couples must make choices about where and with whom to spend these events. Inevitably, one family will feel left out when their son or daughter is spending time with the spouse's family. To alternate festivities or holidays is not a direct affront to the families. The Christmas and Hanukkah traditions could be alternated from year to year, whereas treating Thanksgiving with one family as opposed to the other may not hold as much significance. Or, you could have all families together.

When a couple is of different religions, how to celebrate the holidays may pose an entirely new host of problems, notably the challenge of tailoring customs and traditions to an interfaith home. We've discussed the importance of sharing earlier on. Religion is a form of sharing—just on a greater level. While some couples abandon their religion all together, some people may not be willing to make such a sacrifice. Instead they find a way of sharing religion and holidays in the home. Martha Meyerson, who was raised Catholic, and her husband, Andy, who is Jewish, have accommodated both traditions in their lives, especially after the birth of their first daughter, Kyra. Martha offers some of the following recommendations:

- Expose your children to both customs. Decorate your home with the trimmings of each holiday.
- Partake in the customs of each family.
- Educate your children on the rituals and traditions of each religion.

DO'S

1 Do try to find a balance when adjusting to a new lifestyle with your spouse.

2 Do make compromises when sharing.

3 Do be considerate of the other sex's needs when sharing a bathroom.

4 Do treat joint finances with serious caution.

5 Do make an effort to get along with your spouse's friends and family.

6 Do develop a system for how to spend the holidays with both sets of families.

DON'TS

(1) Don't maintain the same routine when married you had when you were single.

(2) Don't keep your home the same way it was with an ex-spouse when a new partner moves in.

(3) Don't hoard the closet space. Be creative in finding ways to stow your belongings together.

(4) Don't avoid discussing all financial matters and scenarios.

(5) Don't argue with your in-laws on every issue.

(6) Don't deny your spouse's traditions if he is of a different religion.

IN LIVING MATRIMONY QUIZ

In today's society, a prenuptial agreement:
- A. Is more commonplace.
- B. Is outdated.
- C. A sign that your fiancé is having doubts.
- D. None of the above.

ANSWER: A

Handling a prenuptial is best done by:
- A. The fiancé.
- B. The family of the fiancé.
- C. A lawyer.
- D. A friend or proxy.

ANSWER: C

When a couple decorates a home:
- A. The man should stay out of it.
- B. They should work together and not make any hasty purchases.
- C. They should choose what's more economical.
- D. They should hire a decorator.

ANSWER: B

If you're having difficulty sharing a bed with your new spouse, you should:
- A. Ask your doctor for a prescription for sleeping pills.
- B. Give it a while until you make the adjustment.
- C. Subtly kick your partner until he falls off the bed.
- D. Speak to your spouse and find a viable solution.

ANSWER: D

A sensible approach to sharing personal moneys without having any major disagreements is:

    A. To invest in stocks.

    B. Hold separate personal accounts.

    C. Keep a joint checking account.

    D. Avoid discussing how much money you have.

ANSWER: B

A wife who doesn't work should:

    A. Get an allowance.

    B. Be paid per household duty.

    C. Get a job to cover her expenses.

    D. Ask her husband for money when appropriate.

ANSWER: A

Expert Advice

Cokie Roberts, Political Commentator

Having More Faith

Since 1966, Cokie Roberts, the award-winning reporter for ABC television and NPR, has been married to Steve Roberts, a journalist for more than thirty years and well-known commentator on radio and television who regularly appears on various news programs. The Robertses have written From This Day Forward, *a book of stories about their marriage and other American marriages, all told from first-person accounts. They also write a nationally syndicated newspaper column anchored in the* New York Daily News *and are contributing writers to* USA Weekend.

Marriage between a Catholic and a Jew was much more unusual thirty years ago than it is today. As we struggled then with a wedding ceremony that would make both families feel included, little did we know that the choices we made in our early twenties would serve as a metaphor for the marriage ahead. It served us well that we had to deal with serious issues before we married. From the beginning we needed to respect each other, each other's religions, and work through differences before we made the commitment.

That sense of respect goes a long way over the years. Sometimes you'll hear couples talking to each other, or to their children, in a way they wouldn't talk to any other single human being. And it's not pleasant. Good manners aren't something to put in the drawer and pull out just for strangers.

Steve likes to joke: "You can tell the success of your marriage by the number of teeth marks on your tongue." Bite that tongue! Don't say the first thing that comes to mind. In the name of being honest, people are often self-indulgent, hurtful, and mean. We're not endorsing lying here. Obviously, dishonesty can ruin a relationship. But a little tact can go a long way. So can a little charity, and a lot of patience. Then there's listening, as opposed to talking, also a much-underrated trait. Much of this wisdom has taken years to acquire, but we were lucky enough to learn some of those lessons when we were very young. Because we had to talk through, and listen through, what we were going to do about religion, it served as a blueprint for the future.

That future always included observance of both Catholicism and Judaism in our home. We've loved learning each other's traditions, we've relished the celebrations. Our kids thought it was a great deal to get presents at both Hanukkah and Christmas. Now our children are married, and both traditions were represented at their weddings. In fact, our daughter married a Protestant, so celebrants of three religions performed the ceremony—it was like a political ticket. So, all in all, it's worked out well. After a season of cooking and shopping and wrapping forty-some presents for Hanukkah dinner and fifty-some for Christmas dinner, I sometimes sing a different tune. But not for long.

CHAPTER X

FAMILY MATTERS

*F*amily may be life's greatest reward. No, I am not establishing a platform to run for office—that would *never* happen. I am addressing how to handle the intricacies that bring a family together. It is a great challenge to get along with those closest to you and survive unscathed, or survive long enough so that you are not left for hours on a therapist's chair in a hopeless state. However, the pleasure one gains from a courteous and harmonious family life is well worth the work that goes into it.

Etiquette among family members is as, if not more, important to uphold than etiquette in the world at large. It is sensible to assume that you can let your guard down with family members; however, there are rules that need still apply. While it may seem past century, the standard remains that parents are the guardians of their children, and are responsible for setting the example. Within this matrix, there are bound to be circumstances that will present difficulties. If we can remember to handle each situation with grace and courtesy, it may make everyone's life easier.

The Importance of Time

Gone are the days of lunch boxes lovingly packed with quarter-cut sandwiches and a note from Mom. Now that two working parents are the household norm, having only ten minutes to do more than ten things means creativity does not come in the form of lunch-box preparation. Creativity is being able to get your kids off to school in matching socks while guzzling your morning cup of coffee. Time is a luxury that should be futuristically bottled to enhance the lives of us all. Until then we must balance the practical needs of our family with the emotional ones. If you know your child likes the grape juice box over cranberry, be sure to pack the grape. This simple gesture is not only one of respect for your child's likes and dislikes (kids are people, too, remember!), it also lets your child know that even though life gets busy, you still remember him and you still care.

The Dinner Table

Every home should try to enforce some Q.T. (Quality Time). One of the most important rules in twenty-first century etiquette is to instill courteous manners to the younger generation—without imposing too much pressure on them, for they are the upholders of future civility. The best venue to bring family members together without interruptions is to lure them through food, notably at the dinner table, which should be designated as mandatory family time. Don't opt out of this crucial event. All family members should make every effort to make dinnertime work by adjusting schedules if necessary. If you have to miss a night, try to make up that time. Also, catch yourself before an occasional late night at the office or evening event becomes habit. Avoid any distractions that may come up at this time. Don't answer the phone, and leave the television off.

Once you have everyone at the table, dinnertime should be restricted to pleasant conversation. If a parent looks across the table and sees a sullen stare on her teenager, the parent might consider the fact that he is sullen because he has come to expect parental pressure about grades, hairstyle, etc., during the meal. I'm not suggesting such issues shouldn't be dealt with, but have these graver discussions privately. Children should learn that mealtime is a social, anticipated time, while parents are responsible for keeping the tone upbeat.

My reason for placing such dramatic importance to the dinner table is that the family is guaranteed to be together at this time despite the chaos that composes the rest of everyone's days. At an early age, this opportunity for closeness can set the pattern for your family's relations. Everything needs to be considered in preserving this forum. My faith in the future is packaged in my grandchildren. No matter who has a soccer game or play date, they all make it for dinner.

What Every Kid Should Know at the Table

If you are going out to eat, a family-friendly environment should be considered. However, all kids must be able to practice good table manners—whether they're dining at a McDonald's, a four-star restaurant, or at home. Remember, a child's age will dictate what he or she can be expected to handle in terms of manners at the table. Here's general a breakdown:

Ages 3–6: Children this age require patience, as they're just learning the basics. Keep a close eye on them throughout the meal and remind them as to what will not be accepted at the table (slurping, playing with or picking up food with their fingers). Don't indulge them even while they may want to slip or try to test you.

Ages 6–9: You should expect more of an eight-year-old than a three-year-old. All children in this group should know how to eat with a knife and a fork, drink out of a glass properly, put a napkin on their lap, and ask to be excused. If they want to order something else, they should know whom to ask for it.

Ages 10–preteen: At this point, if they don't know their manners, it's time to register them in a teenage table manner–training program.

New Mommy Etiquette

Mothers with small children should be granted every courtesy due to their added, unpredictable bundles. If a small child suddenly acts up, it may not be in the mother's control, and a passerby needs to respect that. By the same token, new mothers should be respectful of the atmosphere into which they take their children, as kids are not always appropriate in adult settings, notably certain restaurants, social gatherings, and professional meetings. Also, I must say I'm astonished by how many mothers I see who use their children's strollers as bumpers on crowded sidewalks.

Mommy and Me Classes

At Mommy and Me classes, all focus needs to be on your child and on the teacher's instruction. Socializing should not occur during class time. It is disruptive for other class members, and prevents you and your child from listening to the teacher. If you want to speak with other mothers, arrive early or stay late to chat. Also, it's a good idea to get to know other new mothers by creating play groups and inviting them and their children over to your home.

Parents should also come to these classes prepared. A mother should have all of the essentials to accommodate her child in her handbag or diaper bag, notably a diaper change and a plastic bag that can be sealed to dispose of the diaper. Never bring a sick child to a class; most Mommy and Me courses have makeup policies.

Sharing

Sharing is a big problem in my grandchildren's house. You give one child a toy and all of the others want it. Time allotment may work, but small children have difficulty understanding the concept of five minutes. Generally, what I do is to show the toyless child the value of something else, perhaps begin a game with him. Or, you could try mother-of-five Ann Jones's approach. Says Jones: "I brainwashed them. Ad nauseam, I would reiterate 'We love to share, don't we?'"

There are also added benefits to sending your child to preschool at an early age, where they learn social and sharing skills.

The Only Child

My daughter hated being an only child, which may be why she now has four kids! I thought life would be easier for her as an only child because she wouldn't have to share with a sibling and had more attention from her parents. Her dissatisfaction as an only child just proves that sharing, as difficult it is, does have great rewards. Because sharing really needs to be learned as a child, preschool is also a good consideration for only children.

In order not to spoil Elena, I tried to be vigilant about not always saying yes each time she wanted something. She was still given household chores and responsibilities. Only children also tend to grow up faster—it is almost inevitable that they will become friends with their parents. While maturity has its benefits, you also want to keep the kid in the kid. Every child needs to relate to what the other kids are experiencing, otherwise they may miss out on something from growing up, always searching for their beloved Rosebud.

Sibling Rivalry

My sister and I fought like heathens. For parents who worry about their kids' penchant for pulling hair and leaving teeth marks, not to worry; Anne (my younger sibling) and I couldn't be closer now. She never *really* did anything to deserve such vicious treatment. Sibling rivalry is a natural stage in childhood.

While it's quick for a parent to routinely punish one of the children involved in a misdeed, it's not necessary to take it too far or make the punishment too severe. You also don't want to encourage your children to get away with tattling, since nobody likes a tattler. The beauty of children is that they have the attention span of an Irish setter—it's not in their nature to prolong a fight or hold a grudge, especially when the latest toy is available to them. This is something we adults can learn from.

Ann Dexter-Jones, who has two twin girls, Samantha and Charlotte, says that her twins have always been and still are incredibly close. "Samantha loved to horseback ride," says Jones. "I never realized until they were much older that Charlotte loved to ride, too. When I asked her why she never pursued it and seemed to prefer other activities, her reply was that Samantha was so happy to visit the stables, so she chose things that she could make special for her, allowed riding to be Samantha's 'thing.' " Sometimes children will surprise you, finding a way to not compete with one another, adds Jones.

Dealing with a Bully

There's always that school bully who torments the other children to the point of such fear, they may not want to tell an adult. If your child continues to come home with a missing belonging, tousled hair, or the occasional war wound, these are subtle indications that he is the target of a bully. Sometimes a child will not be forthright with his extracurricular problem—out of embarrassment and possibly even threats—so it is the parent's responsibility to be aware. Speak to your children. Ask them indirect questions, such as which kids in the class continue to get into trouble and, additionally, which kids are the teacher's favorites. Whenever possible, you should also take your kids to school so you can learn the faces and dynamic of your child's class.

The teacher has a certain amount of responsibility toward your child's well-being, both inside and outside of the classroom. The teacher needs to get involved if your child is the victim of a bully. A parent needs to set a private meeting with the teacher so that she can attend to the matter carefully. The teacher should always be the disciplinarian in such cases. The parent should not take it upon herself to discipline the bully. If the teacher doesn't adequately address the problem, parents should go to the principal.

Taking Your Kids to Public Places

Who hasn't been to a restaurant where the child at the next booth is playing duck, duck, goose on your head? While some parents may consider
their child's behavior adorable, it's not. It's always a treat to go out as a family, but children need to realize that when they are out in public, they must
be on their best behavior. In a store, church, restaurant, or anywhere else
where they are exposed to other people, your child needs to understand
how to act courteously. If your child does act up, you should never severely
punish her in public, but rather take her aside and firmly express the
wrongdoing and attend to discipline at the appropriate time.

Tantrums in Public Places

I know of a mother whose child had such a fit while trying on clothes, that
the entire department store was soon focused on the child's display of tem-
per and tears. When she finally quieted the child down, she said to him in a
nice loud voice, "Wait until I tell your mother!"

The woman was desperate, but unless your child's head spins around and ejects weird green liquid, you should never be ashamed of your child—your responsibility is to him or her, not the public. A child can become out of control from exhaustion or confusion. It is up to a calm adult to regain control. Just witness the parent who gets as riled up as the child and what that accomplishes.

If you feel yourself beginning to lose it, take a step back and allow your child to scream until you have regained composure. Then remove your child from wherever the tantrum is occurring.

Parents Who Reprimand Their Children in Public Places

We've all had the misfortune to stumble upon a parent losing control and berating his child. The parent has obviously overreacted to the child's misbehavior and is having a tantrum of his own. Don't interfere by criticizing and reprimanding the parent. Righteous indignation has no place here.

Parents Who Fight in Front of Their Children

It is a selfish and disrespectful act for parents to fight in front of their children. Not only is this a sorry message to give, but it also upsets the kids. Eventually they will only blame themselves for their parents' quarrels, which could be the worst imposition put on a child.

If you do feel an argument brewing with your spouse, try not to use harsh words. Speak to your spouse reasonably or, ideally, wait for a private moment to speak. Also be sure that your children are out of listening range and can't overhear the argument.

The Quick Fix

I am just waiting for someone to invent the robotic nanny. Essentially, that's been the function that video games and computers provide. Today's technological advancements have such a wondrous effect in occupying your children's attention. It's a luxury to be able to slip away and reacquaint yourself with the life you once knew. However, a parent must be mindful in becoming too overly dependent on such diversions before the kids lose sight of the benefits from building a Lego castle, reading a book, or getting exercise from riding a bicycle. It's similar to appeasing your child each time he craves a piece of candy by giving him a piece of fruit or healthier snack. Sure there will be more negotiating and whimpers to contend with by not always giving them what they want, but maybe they'll thank you for it someday. Ah, the challenges of parenting.

Discipline

It happens. Sometimes a child can express such rage, you may wonder who carried the angry gene. According to Dr. Jonathan Stern, a child psychologist in Manhattan, if a child is harmful physically—by throwing things, pinching, pulling hair, or causing harm to siblings, themselves, or others—such acts deserve disciplinary action. For a younger child, after he exceeds a number of fair warnings, call for a "Time Out." This is a behavioral consequence where you isolate the child by either seating him on a chair that faces the wall, a staircase, or other designated area. It's an effective discipline that teaches emotional self-control. Stern also says that there is no such thing as a bad child, so you can stop looking for the three sixes on your child's scalp. Anger is a result of the parents and environment—so you can look for the three sixes on your own head.

A punishment my mother gave to my sister and me was writing. Like Bart Simpson scribbling on the blackboard, we'd have to write out our misbehavior 100 times. By the fiftieth line, our tiny hands began to hurt. However, you want a child to enjoy writing. By making it a discipline, you give it a negative connotation. When a child dramatically misbehaves, either send her to her room, take her toys away, or institute the words "Time Out." I even bought my grand-kids a bench that has the words "Time Out" written on it.

Past Century/ Present Century

Remember that scene in The Sound of Music *where the children performed like circus entertainers for the guests at an extravagant dinner party? For children to be displayed, not heard, is as outdated as wearing lederhosen for play clothes. At dinner parties, children should be able to mingle politely and un-obtrusively with adult guests. They can even assist a busy host as knowledgeable resources on the home's function—pass-ing hors d'oeuvres, clearing the table, tak-ing coats, etc. However, children shouldn't be required to mingle or serve for the en-tire evening. You may find that your child and guests all enjoy one another, but don't be surprised if your child escapes to the television room to watch a video.*

Responsibility

Put your kids to work. Not only will you have little helpers that can do some additional housework for you, but you'll also teach them the importance of responsibility. By having chores and being rewarded with an allowance, they will re-ceive an early introduction to lifelong employment responsi-bilities.

Assigning your children tasks also demonstrates that you trust them, whether it's picking up a quart of milk or having them look after a younger brother or sister (with supervision, of course—who knows what kind of care my sister would have received if my parents left me alone with her).

Teaching Your Children About Death

Giving your child a pet fish is not only a great way to teach him about responsibility, but since fish don't really live that long, it can also help him understand death. (They're also easier to take care of than hamsters.)

I bought my granddaughter a fish that lived for six months. When it died, she buried it in the garden. If, perchance, there is a death in the family, the child's experience with the fish may help him or her better understand the concept of death. An elementary example that no one, nothing, lasts forever.

Swearing and Naughty Words

"My kids just love the word *sex,*" says Marie Sainsbury, an elementary school teacher, referring to her first-grade students. "They love to repeat naughty words, which are usually words they don't know the meaning of—mainly because they know it's forbidden." Adds Sainsbury, the more she makes a fuss of their saying the words, the more likely they are to continue saying them, "testing me to see how far I will go before I get extremely upset. It's just best not to encourage them."

Children are going to hear swear words no matter how hard you try to avoid using them. It is the adult's responsibility to make them understand beyond a doubt that swear words are careless and inconsiderate.

The Nanny Factor

Hiring the person who nurtures, fosters, and shapes your child's well-being is a task that should be taken very seriously. I would never trust my grandchildren alone with a nanny in her first few weeks with the children. One of the parents should spend this time with the nanny, so that she has an opportunity to learn your views on child care.

Once the child has been released into the nanny's care, parents need to check in with the nanny regularly, even speak to the children. Parents need to be constantly reachable via cellular phone or beepers. The parent is still ultimately responsible for the child's well-being. If it makes you feel more secure and you can afford them, you may wish to install surveillance cameras in your home.

It's only natural that your children will become closely attached to their nanny. A good nanny will most certainly become a part of your family. Don't be intimidated by your children's dependency on the nanny—they know that you are their mommy and daddy—but rather be pleased that your children are in dependable, safe care.

Gay Parenting

For the child who arrives in the school yard with two daddies or two mommies, it's inevitable that the other children will initially mark them as different. Dr. Stern feels that gay parents must be aware of the difficulties that can arise in such circumstances and that it is imperative for them to speak to their child or children at the latest by the age of six or seven to express to them that they have a unique and special family situation. The child should also be prepared for how to respond to the inevitable questions of his peers. For example, if a classmate asks the child, "Why don't you have a mommy?" the child of gay fathers can respond, "Because my parents are daddies." The answer is true and to the point. A teacher should also naturally be aware of the situation to make the adjustment as normal as possible.

Single Parenting

Though I don't encourage single parenting, there's no denying that there are more single parents in today's society. For some, having a child on their own is a conscious decision. For others, circumstances may not be so auspicious. Unfortunately, a single parent may still encounter some resistance in our society. And this resistance may be found from those closest to home. However, the best parents aren't necessarily found in the traditional model.

As Cuba Gooding Junior's character said in *Jerry Maguire,* "Single mothers are a sacred thing." A parent who chooses to raise a child on her own is, from the beginning, establishing how important a child is to her. These parents should be respected for their commitment.

Divorced Parenting

If you are a divorced parent, it's important that you try to get along with your ex-spouse, even if your emotions tell you otherwise. This may require a bit of acting on your part, but it's not fair to involve your children in your personal disputes with the other parent.

Scheduling the children's visits should also be done privately, but allow your kids to voice their preferences and help them consider a routine that works well for them. Be aware whether changes to this routine will interfere with their lives and activities, such as soccer practice and dates with friends. Once the children are old enough to have social lives of their own, parents have to be even more flexible. Friends will no doubt begin to take precedence, and a visiting parent may not have as much appeal as the party of the year that all their friends will be going to. It's important at this time to maintain a fairly regular routine, but try to be flexible on certain occasions as well.

DO'S

1. Do uphold manners with your own family members.
2. Do teach your kids how to use manners in public places.
3. Do make sure that your kids can't overhear an argument with your spouse.
4. Do give your children chores to teach them responsibility.
5. Do make an effort to get along with your ex-spouse, especially when the children are involved.

DON'TS

1. Don't get in the habit of missing family dinners.
2. Don't take your children to inappropriate grown-up places.
3. Don't be overly concerned when siblings fight with one another.
4. Don't punish your kids in public.
5. Don't interfere when a parent reprimands her child in public.

FAMILY MATTERS QUIZ

Dinner table discussions:
    A. Should be kept pleasant.
    B. Should be a forum to discuss serious matters.
    C. Should be educational.
    D. All of the above.
ANSWER: A

For new mothers, Mommy and Me classes:
    A. Are a great way to meet other moms.
    B. Breaks up an otherwise uneventful day.
    C. Are an important learning venue for your child and should be treated seriously.
    D. Any of the above.
ANSWER: C

If a child is the target of the school bully, a parent should:
    A. Instruct the child on how to defend himself.
    B. Call the bully's parents.
    C. Confront the bully.
    D. Inform the child's teacher.
ANSWER: D

If your child throws a tantrum in public, you should:
    A. Apologize to any surrounding people.
    B. Remove your child from wherever the tantrum is occurring.
    C. Discipline the child immediately.
    D. Ignore the child.
ANSWER: B

A child should be disciplined if he:
- A. Throws things.
- B. Causes harm to siblings or others.
- C. Causes harm to himself.
- D. All of the above.

ANSWER: D

When a young child uses a swear word, he should:
- A. Be severely punished.
- B. Have his mouth washed out with soap.
- C. Be given a long, serious talk.
- D. Not be indulged too much by your concern.

ANSWER: D

Gay parents should:
- A. Not distinguish their family situation by having a special talk with their kids.
- B. Discuss the situation with their children when they are old enough to understand.
- C. Reiterate to their kids that they are not like other families.
- D. None of the above.

ANSWER: B

CHAPTER XI

TUNING TEEN ETIQUETTE

*H*ere lies the next generation of etiquette practitioners—take this seriously! As adolescence is a confusing adjustment, and rebellion shapes a preteen's persona the way resilience does a preschooler, they are (and are likely to disagree with this) in need of some life practice before being given the responsibilities of an adult. For parents to be respected, they need to define their role to their children early on. Nothing can be assumed, so a healthy dialogue between parents and kids is key.

Long-term trust and respect will bring a family closer. This comfort level will not only make it easier for adolescents to conduct themselves courteously, it also makes home life less of a battleground. Any household that has a teen in it is bound to face some rough patches. Take heart. Remember that your friends who tell you how perfect their teenage daughter is are probably lying.

There's no doubt the issues today are complicated and it's difficult to know where to start with young adults. And how do you punish the child who now has a good four inches over you and a season of wrestling without having him whack you one?

Try to reason each situation without being overly critical. Rationalize the problem and outline the possible repercussions.

Parents should also be open and honest about specific concerns they have, be it a problem friend the teen is spending time with or the possibility the teen may be experimenting with drugs or alcohol. While teens may view their parents' attitude as very past century, it's important that all sides are understood. It's possible that they may adopt your way.

Kids Today

I find it remarkable that a woman at my age can pick up a few computer tricks from my six-year-old granddaughter, Charlotte. Before I dwell on just how truly frightening this phenomenon is, consider the child who is ten years older than Charlotte. This generation is often light-years ahead of its elders when it comes to knowledge of today's advanced technology. For the know-it-all teen who realizes that he has a few skills over Mom and Dad, that kind of power could have a negative effect. Hubris could lead him to a lack of respect toward his disciplinarians. For the child who feels her advanced knowledge entitles her to advanced privileges, challenging her parents and authoritative persons, she needs to be softly put in her place. Just gently say, "I don't necessarily agree with you. Why don't we see if we can work things out before I have to become a *real* parent."

Overly Involved Parents

We make our own bed and sleep in it—but it's your bed to make. You don't want to make a teenager's bed, literally or figuratively. I'd first like to admit from personal experience that we all make mistakes. It's hard as a parent not to want to be involved in every aspect of your child's life—no matter what his age. However, it's important for a parent to let go and to try to step away no matter how difficult this may seem. Trust me, I know how hard it is. Just ask my daughter, who has children of her own, how much I've improved in not rearranging her house each time I visit her. Still, children at any age deserve space to themselves and we as parents must respect that.

Teens and the Internet

The Internet is a wonderful tool for the academic and worldly information it can expose your child to. This is also the same technology that can teach your child how to build a bomb. While limited access may be one consideration to avoid this problem, keep in mind that such limits may eventually only fuel the child's curiosity. A curious child will stop at nothing to satisfy that curiosity. Limiting access will only cause the child to pursue curiosities in secret. So how do you harness their exposure to controversial mediums? One of the best things for a relationship between teens and parents, however awkward, is to maintain open dialogue. Be aware and accepting of your child's needs and current influences and openly discuss the evils of society. Remember the child who could never have sweets and then gained thirty pounds in college when she could eat grilled cheese sandwiches and Oreos whenever she wanted? Just add the most harmful Internet sites to the scenario and your child may be discussing his harms on *The Jerry Springer Show.*

Teens and the Telephone

Along with getting a driver's permit and going on his first date, chatting on the phone and e-mail is part of the teenager's livelihood. It's a wonder how your kids can spend all day with friends at school and then come home and spend hours in the evening bantering back and forth on the phone or computer. As a result of their need to be updated what may seem hourly on their friends' lives both on the phone and online, a household can be disrupted. A home with a teenager or (gasp) *teens* should have regulations that may include no receiving or making calls after a certain hour and designated Internet access time for each member of the family.

To families that can afford an extra phone line, I say have it installed. While it may appear as a luxury to the teen, it's really the parents who will benefit—reveling in being undisturbed. Here are some rules that families may consider implementing:

- Institute a phone message system—either a pad or a chalk-board by the phone.
- Be certain to save or write down any messages from the answering machine.
- No one should pick up a line and address any questions when someone is in the midst of a conversation.
- Parents should respect a teenager's right to privacy and not listen in to a phone conversation or read their child's e-mail.

Swearing Among Teens

Teenagers often use obscenities among themselves but know to clean up their language when in the presence of adults. If you are concerned that your child will not make the distinction—make it for them.

When Your Child's Friend Is Rude

If your child's friend complains about the lack of videos to choose from or about the food being served, it's certainly not your child's fault. Sometimes a teenage guest is uncomfortable or used to the disciplines of his own home. Rather than forbid your child from seeing their peer—which can only lead to a rebellious quarrel on your teen's part—make sure that your child discusses with his friends the rules of your household before he has guests over.

The Problem Friend

There's always that one problem friend—the one who's a little too smug for her own good, seems to live in a house run like a nightclub, and whose eyes always seem a little glazed over. The naughty kid always seems to have a lot of friends, and once your child is enlisted into her coterie, it's only natural for a parent to be concerned for fear that their child will adapt to her bad ways. However, you can't forbid your children from seeing their friends. The more my parents harped on why I couldn't associate with the problem friend, the more I wanted to be with her—it only got worse. It's natural that your child will want to defend her friend. Again, talk honestly to your child about your concerns without accusing him of mimicking the friend's behavior. Let your child know you trust him to make the right choices even when you're not there to supervise.

Embarrassing Your Kids

Teenagers are so worried about how others perceive them that being labeled as different for any reason can seem devastating. My parents embarrassed me constantly with their formal lifestyle. Kids are critical of one another, and parents need to be aware of this.

A parent may think that hauling out her child's ducky baby blanket in front of peers is cute and harmless—but to the child, it's probably not.

It's acceptable for children to tell parents privately that some of their actions may embarrass them. And parents shouldn't feel hurt, but rather appreciate their children's efforts in trying to be open and honest. Some parents let their kids get away with too much, however. You're still the parent, and they need to respect you. Establish boundaries and what you are willing to tolerate as appropriate behavior.

Teens and Trends

If your child comes home in the latest shade of blue—blue hair, that is—rather than treat his odd choice in hair coloring as an act of rebellion, look at it as his form of experimentation. And experimenting with hair dyes is a lot safer than stronger substances that can cause more damage than just abusing hair follicles. Teenagers spend an enormous amount of time trying to simultaneously fit in with their peers and distinguishing themselves from everyone else in the world.

If you were to punish your child for such typical teen behavior, you may discover that it will induce her to rebel even more. Tell her, "That's an interesting hairstyle—what prompted you to make such a drastic decision?" This gently demonstrates your disapproval while, more importantly, gives your child the opportunity to speak openly about her decision. There is even a strong possibility that she may not even like her latest look, but it's just a way for her to speak openly about her confusion toward experimentation. It is important for your child, now more than ever, to be shown compassion and understanding rather than be reprimanded for her choices.

Makeup

It's interesting how a daughter may begin wearing her makeup as if it was applied with a paint roller and then, later in life, abandon it altogether but for a neutral lipstick and some powder. A mother rarely gets her way on this issue.

Some girls will show an interest in cosmetics when they are small children watching their mothers in awe as they get ready for an evening out, while others will never become particularly interested. If she is the former, I think at fourteen she is old enough to wear a little lipstick and eye makeup when she leaves the house. If she is wearing too much, her friends may tell her. It's important to remember that makeup can be bad for your skin, creating even more problems to sensitive skin types. Visiting a makeup counter and learning from a cosmetologist the types of products that work best for her skin can not only be fun but helpful.

Borrowing the Car

Imagine the parent that gets into the car on Monday morning only to find the radio tuned—very loudly—to a hip-hop station, no gas in the tank, and the dependable umbrella missing from under the seat. What parent wouldn't come to the definite conclusion that his child will never drive the family car again?

Teenagers must understand that borrowing the car is a privilege, not a right, and this privilege should have a few rules attached to it, such as:

- Fill the tank (or at least replace the gas used).
- Reset the radio stations and turn the volume to a reasonable level.
- Leave the car the way you found it.
- Clean up, including under the seats and the ashtrays.
- Pay tickets immediately, or better yet, take the time to find a legal parking space.
- Park the car in safe areas.

Establishing a Curfew

The curfew is the parents' decision; however, I feel it should be based on what is the normal time in your community. Have a discussion with your child so you can establish a happy medium, but let your child know that yours shall be the final decision.

If your child will be late, it is mandatory that he call. You can discuss the details on why he was unable to make the curfew in the morning.

A curfew is sometimes extended on certain evenings—on prom night, for example—and you'd be foolish to try and wait up. The curfew is usually discontinued after high school.

Teens and Substance Abuse

If only blue hair was all that your child came home with. One of the worst fears a parent of a teen may have is that his child is experimenting with cigarettes, alcohol, or—even worse—drugs.

Although the legal drinking age in most states is twenty-one, to assume that your child will wait until then to take his first sip of alcohol would be, to put it mildly, delusional. Most teenagers don't obey state liquor laws. They experiment based on seeing most of their friends and elders using alcohol and drugs, wanting to find out for themselves what the effects are. Such experimentation is usually harmless; however, some can abuse it.

If you suspect that your child is using drugs, look for the signs. Do the research—speak to friends, teachers, and regard her behavior more closely. If your assumption is realized, as a parent you have the right to employ the search and seize method. The intentions are for your child's best. Sitting back and wondering if your child is okay can only exasperate her problems, when she really needs help.

Drugs and Alcohol at Parties

When my daughter was fourteen, she went to a party that was chaperoned by an older brother and sister who were more interested in watching *Saturday Night Live* than in supervising their younger sister's party. When the liquor and drugs appeared, my daughter and many of her friends left. They were frightened that the party had gotten out of control.

Until kids are eighteen years old, parties should be supervised by adults who will make sure the event is kept running smoothly. Not only could there be sketchy behavior at the party resulting from substance abuse, but, even more important, someone under the influence could get behind the wheel of a car. Driving while intoxicated is a leading killer of teenagers today.

It's not improper etiquette as much as it is against the law to serve alcohol to teens at parties. If your party is visited by a few swaggering, slurring guests who thank the family dog for hosting such a swell party, be sure that a sober guest drives them home or surrender a room in the house as a safe haven for the night. It's your responsibility that inebriated guests not drive home. The host's next responsibility is to contact the parents of the teenagers who have had too much to drink and to explain that they will be spending the night.

Dating

Kids in their early teens soon discover that the opposite sex no longer holds the icky stigma of being cootie-bearing specimens that they once did. As parents will soon discover, their sons won't be getting calls from just boys any longer, and their little girls are more interested in what a certain boy likes over Dad's once revered opinions. Children in their early teens usually begin to go out together in groups. When "real" dating should begin is a bone of contention in some families. Parents usually set this time themselves, since an arbitrary age does not take into account the maturity of their child, along with the social customs of their community. The first-date dilemma was solved for one set of anxious parents when the boy whom their daughter had a special crush on asked her for the first date, which was at a dinner where his parents would be in attendance. Possibly the boy's parents were a bit anxious, too, and wanted to meet the girl their son had talked so much about.

Parents meeting their children's dates

When a boy calls for a girl at her home, beeping the horn and waiting for her in the car won't do. He needs to come to the door. If he hasn't yet met her parents, she should introduce him and spend time making conversation. Cross-examinations are not necessary, but hopefully the boy will be forthcoming in filling in anxious parents about the particulars of the date. Otherwise parents are right to ask where they will be, and at what time she can be expected home. Parents also need to do their part to not embarrass their child during this highly awkward moment. Needless to say, any remarks about how adorable it is that their daughter is now entering adulthood need to be saved for when the date is absent.

The Sex Talk

There is no set age when your child will broach the facts-of-life conversation. If your preteen hasn't demonstrated a willingness to discuss the subject, don't presume that she already knows the deal. Even in the most liberal of households, a child could be shy when it comes to specific questions regarding sexuality. While sex-education classes being taught in schools and religious organizations are a far more superior method to learning about sex on the street, it's hard to really determine if your child is getting the immediate answers to her questions. In other words, assume nothing. Instead, initiate the discussion with an explanation of puberty and the changes boys and girls will experience in their bodies during those years. Mothers talk with daughters, and fathers with sons, so questions can be answered with accuracy and little embarrassment. Single parents may ask a friend or family member of the same sex as her child to speak with the child.

Advice regarding birth control

When your teen starts dating regularly, and especially one boyfriend or girlfriend exclusively, it's safe to assume that he or she will be considering sex. Therefore it's important to include information on birth control—to prevent diseases and pregnancy—in your earliest discussions about sex with your child. Attempting this conversation for the first time when your teen is already seriously involved could be construed by your child as an invasion of privacy. It's better to have laid the groundwork before the situation presents itself.

If your daughter brings up the subject of birth control, or if you want to initiate the subject yourself, the best advice is to suggest making an appointment with a gynecologist. The doctor will be more knowledgeable and be able to give more specific, professional information, and your child may be able to ask questions with greater openness. (Naturally, if a parent's religious views do not permit the use of birth control, a parent wouldn't advocate it for a child.)

When a grown child brings a friend of the opposite sex home for a visit

Once your child leaves your home for college, work, or his personal calling, you have little control over his life. When that child returns home for a visit, he's returned to more than a teen-postered room. Things can be awkward for both parents and child as everyone struggles with their new roles. Children should remember that they are visiting *their parents' house.* Therefore, parents set the rules.

While some parents are casual and accepting of their children's independent lifestyle and will put an unmarried couple in the same bedroom, others may always maintain an old-fashioned resilience to this rule. While they are all too aware that their child is sexually active, they don't need to be reminded of it in their own home. Your child may resist your behavior, deeming it hypocritical. To that you should reply, "While in my house, you must abide by my rules."

The Teen and Financial Responsibility

It is important for teenagers to learn financial responsibility, and not assume that you will cover all of their added expenses—for example, CDs, makeup, movie tickets, etc. Go over with them the expenses that you will cover—clothing, food, housing, gas for the car, and anything school- or health-related are all reasonable bills that the adult should tend to.

A parent should also encourage children to take after-school jobs such as baby-sitting. This added income, along with their regular allowance, will help teens learn how to budget their money.

The Teen's First Job Interview

Applying for a first job as a teenager can pose a significant challenge, since most teens don't have enough experience to even fill out a line of a résumé. This is where creative self-promotion comes in. If your child is applying for a job as a camp counselor, suggest that he mention that he's had almost a lifetime of experience looking after two younger brothers. Even the most mundane of household work can be considered important—painting the basement, implementing a recycling system, and computerizing a family's social calendar are all skills that can be used in the outside world.

Let him know that the most important thing he can demonstrate to an interviewer is that he is enthusiastic about the position. Recommend that he ask questions, listen intently, and let the interviewer know that he is not afraid of hard work.

The College Interview

The college interview shouldn't be as scary as the overly anxious parent might make it out to be during the car ride to the university. It can actually be an interesting and enjoyable process, and parents should try to convey this attitude to their nervous kids. An interview is as much an opportunity for the applicant to learn about a school as it is for the professional to learn about the candidate in the short time they have together.

While an applicant's credentials and college essay may be exemplary, a stiff candidate doesn't merit high points. This is also an opportunity for the academically challenged student to shine, addressing his finer skills with charisma and the panache of a successful entrepreneur. A good interview is when the prospective student demonstrates a genuine interest in attending the school and can express what positive qualities he or she will add to campus life. Thus, the interviewee should be prepared, having learned as much about the school's campus, programs, and social life as possible before the interview. A candidate who demonstrates a knowledgeable enthusiasm for the university's offerings will stand out, as opposed to the applicant who based his application decision on the good-looking people featured in the brochure.

After the college visit, make certain that your child saved all of the names and contact information of the people with whom he interviewed. This is to organize thank-you notes. Like a job interview, college admissions staff should receive these notes, which will make your child stand out as an applicant.

DO'S

❶ Do maintain healthy dialogue with your teen.

❷ Do openly discuss the negative influences and taboo subjects that your teens may come across over the Internet.

❸ Do consider implementing a schedule in your house for telephone use.

❹ Do encourage your teenage daughter to come with you to visit a makeup counter if she shows an interest in cosmetics.

❺ Do consider an outside person to confront a teen with a substance abuse problem.

DON'TS

① Don't be overly involved in all of your children's decisions.

② Don't allow your kids to get away with obscene language.

③ Don't give your teen car privileges without implementing rules first.

④ Don't allow your underage teen to go to a party without parental supervision.

⑤ Don't depend on outside programs to teach your children about sex education.

TUNING TEEN ETIQUETTE QUIZ

When establishing rules for the telephone, you should:
  A. Institute a phone message system so everyone in the family is sure to receive all messages.
  B. Honor the privacy of a personal call.
  C. Make it clear that no one should pick up and speak, or listen in on a line that is already engaged.
  D. All of the above.

ANSWER: D

If your child's friend is rude, you should:
  A. Forbid your child from seeing him.
  B. Ask the friend for an apology.
  C. Ask your child to speak with the friend to let him know that you feel his actions were inappropriate.
  D. Speak to the friend's parents.

ANSWER: C

If your child experiments with a fashion trend that you don't particularly like, you should:
  A. Allow her to experiment without your opinions.
  B. Casually mention that you don't find the trend flattering.
  C. Punish the child.
  D. None of the above.

ANSWER: B

If a guest arrives at or attempts to leave your teen's party inebriated, you should:
  A. Have him spend the night and inform his parents.
  B. Call the police.
  C. Let him leave.
  D. End the party.

ANSWER: A

A teenager should begin dating:

    A. At age thirteen.

    B. At age fifteen.

    C. At age seventeen.

    D. When it makes sense based on maturity level and the social customs of the community.

ANSWER: D

The best way to handle birth control for your daughter is:

    A. To forbid the subject entirely.

    B. To leave a brochure in her room.

    C. To make an appointment for her with a gynecologist.

    D. To allow her the freedom to choose whatever method works for her.

ANSWER: C

The primary benefit of a college interview is:

    A. For an interviewer to evaluate the applicant.

    B. To see if the candidate can handle an in-person meeting.

    C. For a candidate to learn about the school.

    D. For the applicant to see the campus.

ANSWER: C

ETIQUETTE DURING LIFE'S CHALLENGES

*L*ife is difficult," aptly begins *The Road Less Traveled*. Being human is learning how to handle life's obstacles—especially the obstacles that are beyond your control. For some, handling daily stress with humor helps, while others who are in times of serious crises may need the support of those closest to them. Difficult times require everyone to act with extra sensitivity and grace. It is times like these when treating others with decency is of utmost importance.

Handling Tragedy

I've seen people handle tragedy in many different ways. Some shut down and pretend the incident never happened, while others blame the world for their struggle. It's only natural to go through a period of behavior that is not in your typical nature, but, at some point, one needs to move on. It's up to you to find an outlet and do what you can in order to get yourself back on track—whether it's looking to your support network, seeking spiritual guidance, or focusing on work or a hobby.

I have a friend who recovered from a life-threatening accident and then lost her husband and daughter. She has had more tests then Job. However, she persevered. She's become an example of strength and poise to me, and I think about her whenever I'm tempted to moan about how bad the traffic is.

If you chronically feel depressed and unable to overcome your situation, consider professional help. The assistance from a therapist can provide the unbiased counseling to pull you through.

How to Handle Other People's Tragedies

Since everyone reacts to problems differently, begin by trying to gauge how much your help is wanted. One should always offer, but don't take it personally if your offer is not accepted. If you don't know the aggrieved person all that well, a polite offer is always courteous. If it's someone close to you, and you really feel she needs your help, you can be more aggressive. If she's not receptive, try: "If I was going through something as equally bad, I would hope that you would help."

Separation/Divorce

Unless a couple is separating under extremely good terms, I recommend that lawyers handle the proceedings whenever possible—particularly when it comes to finances, the root of all things ugly.

Many divorced couples feel as if they are still married, since they often need to be in contact with each other regarding alimony, the mortgage, the kids, etc. Pursuing a new life while maintaining the pragmatics of your former is difficult to juggle. It's up to you to find a comfortable way to make the transition from married person to newly single. You might begin simply by no longer wearing your wedding ring, or you might decide to move to another town or find a new home. Managing a new life may feel like a task that you have completely forgotten how to master. In time, you'll ease into your new life.

Whom and When to Tell

Since the card industry is yet to be known for putting out a line of cards specifically for divorces, alerting acquaintances about your unfortunate news via correspondence is not standard. Whom and when to tell should be considered foremost, especially if you have children. It's a good idea to make an appointment with your children's teachers so they are aware of the situation at home.

Divorced couples usually want to put the marriage behind them, which can be difficult, since friends usually want to bring it up. The problem is trying to manage the line between telling acquaintances nothing, which might hurt them, or telling them too much, which might hurt you. There is also a point when you can belabor the subject.

It's also unfair to expect them to take sides. If you do want to find solace in the comfort of others, be careful not to disparage your ex-spouse, since that is an invitation to awkwardness. Tell coworkers when the time is right, but keep emotions aside—business is business.

New Partner, New Kids

If you're marrying for the second (or, in today's age, third or fourth time), you may be acquiring more than a new spouse—sometimes added children come with the package. Keep in mind this situation is probably more difficult for the children than you, so be respectful of their feelings and patient in making the transition as easy as possible. You can't expect a 360-degree turn in 30 minutes. Life isn't a sitcom. If children act out, it's hard to really blame them. Their perspective is that they already have a mommy or daddy. Any forced relation will only lead to a superficial connection.

If two sets of children are joined under one roof, naturally the children are bound to fight. While it may be instinctive for the parents to come to their own children's defense, try to keep an open mind and remember not to lose sight of the big picture, which is that you are now a single family unit.

Gossip

For those intrigued by the gossip (and, yes, I read Liz Smith), whether the information is true or not, don't feed the frenzy. Gossip about others will inevitably return to the feeble source where it began. If you ever become a victim of incorrect gossip, confront the issue rather than wait for the story to wane until the next scandal. Speak honestly with close friends and family. Your true relations will prevail and carry you through a difficult period.

Private Problems That Become Public

My father always said: "Don't wash your dirty laundry in public." For those times when your dirty laundry becomes everyone's business, keeping a low profile until the incident blows over is always a graceful approach. There is also Mr. Hugh Grant's approach, bravely admitting to his sordid divine pleasures by appearing on *The Tonight Show.* His ability to poke fun at his own offense was a tactic that worked in his favor.

Exposing your side of the story to people who don't know you, unfortunate as it may be, you can never control what others may think of you. This is precisely why, unless you're running for office, you can't be concerned about the opinions of others. And even a former president was able to bypass a little intern scandal. As this is a time where the support of others will be in most need, you'll discover that true friends will prevail.

Losing a Job

Losing a job causes a great amount of emotional as well as financial upheaval. As with any other type of loss, you need to give yourself enough time to mourn. Remember, you will survive this loss and go on to begin a new professional life for yourself.

Whether you are looking for a new job because you were laid off or were just unhappy at your old job, it's always sensible to begin by focusing on what career it is that you really want to pursue. Speaking to contacts and looking at employment listings can help familiarize yourself with what is out there. Try to secure as many interviews as possible, even if they are not all for the exact position that you are seeking. The worst thing that can happen is that the company will have your résumé on file and could call you when an appropriate opportunity becomes available. And any new contacts are always good to have.

Sometimes people who have lost their jobs find that it was the best professional move for them. It can be an impetus in taking that risk and starting the company that you've always dreamed of creating. Or taking a break from the corporate world to finally take those trips you promised yourself. With a change of scenery and environment, you may come to the conclusion that it wasn't just the job that didn't satisfy you, but maybe it's time to relocate. Whatever discovery you make, it's important to be open to change and look at this possible setback as a positive life opportunity.

Since many people in this country tend to measure their careers with their personal successes, being out of work may be a stigma. This is an American concept that is not completely sound. Career, money, and power—while all impressive successes—hardly measure to a balanced, fruitful life. Never underestimate the achievements of intellectual, athletic, humanitarian, or other pursuits that improve the overall quality of life. For the unemployed who feel uncomfortable by their current job status, when asked the inevitable question "What do you do?" simply respond, "I am in between jobs." Or speak politically about how you just began yoga, art classes, or another skill that you are proud of.

Facing Illness

I've had a few friends who have been diagnosed with cancer. One in particular was always extremely strong in spirit during her ordeal. Every time I went to visit her, she always had an "I'll beat it" attitude. I really did believe that she could survive her cancer.

People faced with illness occasionally lose the will to live. Others choose to see things in a different perspective.

Additionally, illness doesn't just affect the one with the ailment, but all who are closest to that person. As hard as it may be, be aware of the sadness of others. It's amazing to realize how your life can touch so many—a lesson so aptly illustrated by George Bailey in *It's a Wonderful Life*.

How to Treat People with Illness

If it is a good friend or close relative who is ill, you should not be afraid to talk openly about the illness. If, however, that person does not want to talk about her disease, she will probably say so. The best thing that you can do is to be there for support.

Hospital Etiquette

A patient in the hospital, if up to it, always appreciates visitors to break up long, depressing days. You should check in with both the hospital and patient before you make a visit, to learn when visiting hours take place and what time is most convenient for the patient. Keep your phone conversations to a minimum, because the patient may be too tired to converse. Also, if the patient is sharing a room, it's unfair to the other person to have to continually hear him on the phone. Before arriving, offer your services. Ask if he needs for you to get his mail, make phone calls, attend to pets, etc.

Tips when visiting a patient in the hospital:

- Make the effort to visit, even if it's for five minutes; your presence is appreciated.
- Don't feel that you have to bring something; it's better to wait until you know what the person needs—for example, magazines or a pack of gum—something the patient really wants.
- Don't bring flowers unless they come in a vase, since many hospitals don't have containers handy for patient use.
- Flower arrangements should be small, since there is not much space in a hospital room.
- Know the correct visiting times.
- Avoid staying too long. Be sensitive to how the patient is feeling.
- There is typically no more than two visitors to a room, and all visitors should abide by hospital rules.
- Keep your voice down, especially if the patient is sharing a room.

Suicide

Suicide is one of those tragedies that is impossible to make sense of. There is often no explanation, just overwhelming sadness. If someone you loved took her life, the comfort of family and friends is an immediate necessity. Seeking professional help is also a good idea.

For friends and family, it is important to acknowledge the suicide. The worst thing to do is just ignore that it ever happened. When my friend Celeste's mother took her life, she couldn't believe how many acquaintances would look at her as if nothing had happened. "Friends should acknowledge that you're hurting and be supportive," says Celeste. "Not look at you as if you are abnormal, but rather look at you as a human being going through a hard period. It puts everyone at ease."

While it's not necessary to pry, and improper to ask for all of the details surrounding the death, it is important to let those grieving understand that you are concerned, aware of their difficult situation, and are there for them.

After Celeste's mother's suicide, when acquaintances simply ignored her, she felt sad and insecure, always feeling that people were saying things behind her back. There were also those people whom she barely knew who became nosy—she automatically felt like an outcast.

As with anyone who is going through a unique situation, it is best not to make the person feel more ill at ease. "If someone asks about my mother, not realizing that she has passed on," says Celeste, "I just say, 'As a matter of fact, she passed away.' If they push the conversation, wanting to know the reason of her death, I reply, 'She had some issues in life. She wasn't really happy.' If I feel comfortable with a person, sensing that he can handle it, I will discuss her suicide. It's a matter of fact."

Notice of Death

Death notices are sent to the papers of the community where the deceased lived. They usually contain the date of death, names of immediate family members, and the place and time of the funeral. Sometimes they will request a contribution to a charity in lieu of sending flowers. The notice will also say if the funeral is private. A death notice may read as follows:

Dowd, Tom, [beloved] husband of Louisa Cotter Dowd and father of Winston and James Dowd. Services Sunday, November 14 at 10:30 A.M. at Saint John and Paul Catholic Church (450 Weaver Street, Larchmont).

Following is an example written by friends and associates:

> Patterson, Mary. We are deeply saddened by the untimely passing and loss of our very dear friend and associate, who was always considered a member of our family. Her wise council will be greatly missed. Our most heartfelt condolences go out to her family and friends.

Funerals

Here's a morbid question: How would you like your funeral to be? Putting a lighter touch to a grave affair, consider the personality of the deceased and how she would have liked her funeral to be celebrated. My father's favorite song was always "When the Saints Come Marching In." At his funeral we had the choir play a rousing rendition of the tune, which I'm sure gave him a chuckle.

When my grandmother Ford passed away, she designated that the church be filled with only white roses. I'll never forget how beautiful the church looked. What was most touching was that the funeral reflected the beauty of the person for whom it was being held—just the way she would have wanted it to be.

As sad as funerals are, they also celebrate a person's life, bringing together the deceased's loved ones as a commemoration. And it's always special to be in the company of people who shared the same love for someone.

When There Are No Right Words

A condolence call or letter is always a thoughtful sentiment. Keep them short. With so many letters one receives, it's a task to get through them all (see Chapter VII, "Correspondence"). When you are in contact with the deceased's loved ones, it's always nice to share a personal experience, recount on how that person touched your life.

It may seem awkward to bring up a death; however, just like the crazy auntie in the attic, it can be even more odd not to. A friend of mine who recently lost her father was grateful that I offered her my condolences. She commented on how uncomfortable it was in that many acquaintances avoided bringing up his passing altogether. My genuine acknowledgment and assistance gave her a moment of happiness during a difficult time.

DO'S

❶ Do find a healthy outlet if you're facing a tragedy.

❷ Do tell your children's teachers that you are going through a divorce.

❸ Do confront the issue when you've become a victim of incorrect gossip.

❹ Do look at a job loss as a new professional opportunity.

DON'TS

① Don't neglect someone's offer for help if you are in need of support.

② Don't be quick to take your children's side when they have disagreements with your new spouse's children.

③ Don't add to gossip.

④ Don't stay on the phone too long when calling a patient in a hospital.

⑤ Don't ignore an acquaintance who lost someone through suicide.

ETIQUETTE DURING LIFE'S CHALLENGES QUIZ

If your scandal becomes public:
- A. Keep a low profile.
- B. Confront the issue tastefully and honestly.
- C. Seek the comfort and advice of those you trust.
- D. Any of the above.

ANSWER: D

When visiting a friend at the hospital, a sensible gesture is to:
- A. Bring flowers.
- B. Come with a big group.
- C. Offer your assistance.
- D. Plan on staying for a long time.

ANSWER: C

Death notices are sent to:
- A. Local papers.
- B. Family and close friends.
- C. Funeral parlors.
- D. Lawyers.

ANSWER: A

Expert Advice

Eddie McGee, *Big Brother* Winner

At No Disadvantage

Edward McGee is the winner of CBS's first Big Brother *competition—a program that televised ten strangers living in a house with no contact to the outside world. McGee is also a cancer survivor. His proudest accomplishment is teaching children that being disabled (having lost a leg from his illness) doesn't mean that you can't live a rewarding life.*

It's pretty surprising that the guy who kept *Big Brother* producers on constant alert (so they could bleep my expletives in time) is included in an etiquette book! Don't come to me for advice on why it's not polite to burp at the table, but in understanding how to educate the public on disabilities—that's something I can understand.

When ABs (Able Bodies) view a handicapped person for the first time, it's inevitable that they'll notice the disability. Ultimately, if they stick around, they get to know the person, see him for who he really is. I suppose that on *Big Brother,* the viewers initially perceived me as "the guy with one leg." Once they came to know my character, my missing leg wasn't as much of a distinguishing factor. The crutches can just melt away—they're like a pair of shoes. It's a good lesson for us all, even people with disabilities.

For the handicapped person coming to terms with his disability, it's only natural that he'll question his undeserved misfortune. The fact is, you're dealt this hand and you have to play it. When I was eleven, in the hospital with cancer, I had the "Why me?" week. Then I had to move on. Luckily, my strong support group—family, little brother—pulled me through. I chose not to live the disabled life and bemoan my hardship. If I weren't disabled, who knows, I could be pumping gas or swigging beers with my friends here in Long Island [where McGee lives]. Now, after earning a scholarship to the University of Texas, I've received an education. I've also learned to not fear taking a situation to its fullest potential. Work within the lifestyle you are given. I occasionally park in the handicapped space without really needing to—and I can get around better than that person who needs to begin a Weight Watchers program.

My focus is to increase handicap awareness, primarily among young disabled children. To educate on the life that you can have after disability. I found my niche in wheelchair basketball, an activity that has most certainly given me a positive disposition. With millions of issues I need to get through, on the basketball court, I can work things out. I try to stress to youngsters to get involved in an activity that will motivate—whether it be the arts, music, sports, whatever makes them happy. By working with nationwide programs such as Handicap Awareness Days, I am in touch with people from ages five all the way up to high school seniors. The message is always the same—get involved. You don't have to be Michael Jordan or Mozart, just find your stimulant.

CHAPTER XIII

DRESS CODE

*I*s purple this season's black, or is punk making more noise than ladylike dressing is? Following fashion can be dizzying. Clothing is not as simple as providing protection and comfort, it's an instant indication of who you are. A music executive may be as turned off by a three-piece suit as a grand dame of Park Avenue would be by body piercing and tattoos. "The clothes you wear give people a fast, clean impression on who you are. It's like having that preconversation," says Hal Rubenstein, Fashion Features Director of *InStyle* magazine.

As style is a form of expression, be cognizant of how it fits into the framework of your life. But also be sure to have fun with fashion; finding your personality through style is something to dress for.

Finding Your Style

Descartes once said: "Know thyself." Whoever knew that he was referring to personal style? Looking fashionable is not about stuffing your closet with the latest trends, but more about being comfortable in clothes that suit you. Whatever style you choose to wear, it's important to feel confident. Finding clothes that flatter your body type and match your lifestyle will help you feel good about yourself and the way you look to the world.

Style is an individual thing. However, some general rules do apply when it comes to presenting oneself in the best light possible. If there's one thing I'd like to get across to many of the women out there, skin tight is not sexy when you have the belly of a Buddha. I know of someone who continually wears leggings and has thighs as big as boulders. Does she see what I see? Well-fitted and tight are two different things. It's up to you to find the cuts and clothes that fit your proportions.

For men, straggly hair with a two-day beard, jeans, and a T-shirt has the American rugged, oh, so handsome Brad Pitt look. But remember who and where you are—this image won't take you to the office.

If you find pieces of clothing that work well on you, make the investment and buy a few of these pieces in different colors and patterns. You'll probably

save in the long run. If you're still in a quandary finding your personal style, shop with your spouse, mother—anyone who will give you a straight opinion. A good salesperson can also assist on sizing, and leading department stores such as Macy's have personal shopping services that can help.

Dressing the Part

How you look is a quick introduction to who you are. For the highly opinionated set out there, this puts the pressure on to send out the appropriate message.

At the New York Presbyterian Hospital in New York City, the doctors and many of the administrative staff all wear suits—maintaining a professional decorum. Like eating a Big Mac at the dining room table, it seems inappropriate to wear jeans and a tank top at the reception desk of a large corporate office. How you look is especially important when it is projecting the image of a company.

If a prospective client walks into a bank, for example, and the staff is dressed in khakis and polo shirts, this image may not work for a conservative investor, but could be a draw to a successful entrepreneur. "The company has to decide whom they want their client to be," says Hal Rubenstein. "We do judge books by their covers. We have been trained to. We look at it about choice. You choose to wear this."

Dressing for the Job Interview

When meeting someone for a job interview, that first impression has to count. On a job interview, no matter how brilliant or charming you may be, you only have so much time to convey your finer qualities. What you wear speaks volumes at first sight.

A little research is required before you walk in for that interview, and I'm not talking only about the company history (although this, of course, is important). You want to wear what's reflective of that business. "Look to the leader. He sets the tone—look to the indicators of that corporate culture," says Christina Gabriel, Director in Relationship Marketing for Banana Republic. "I was wearing almost the same suit as the person interviewing me!" says Joanne Napolitano, who got the job as a producer for *Charlie Rose*. While stalking your interviewer before your meeting in order to wear a similar outfit may be a bit excessive, you should dress as though you are ready to start working on the day of the interview.

If you never met your interviewer, use some psychology. A new media company where your prospective boss probably spends more time at the office than at home will more likely be wearing jeans and a T-shirt. If it's at a hoity-toity fashion magazine, you'll want to show that you are up on the latest styles. Keep in mind that you shouldn't look more casual than the boss and, under no circumstances, should a woman wear a see-through top with a skirt slit up to your . . . well, slit high, unless it's a waitressing job at Hooters.

Dressing in Today's Workplace

New technology isn't just making it possible to buy groceries online—it's also been an impetus to the *casualization* of the workplace. "Dressing down is a costless perk when hiring people for investment jobs," says Terry Corcoran of the investment firm Himalaya Capital. And, since many banks were losing good people to technology companies, firms such as JP Morgan, Salomon Smith Barney, and Goldman Sachs have declared a dress-down policy. However, a dress-down policy at an investment bank is not the same as one at a dot-com. You must keep in mind the nature of the business you're in. Hal Rubenstein, who wears a suit to the office despite the casual environment at *InStyle* magazine, is comfortable with his look because it is appropriate to the nature of his work. "I represent fashion and am in contact with professionals in the business," he says. It is important to think about what types of interactions you will have throughout the day. Do you take potential clients out to lunch and try to sell yourself and your business? Are you an architect visiting construction sites? These situations call for very different attire. The leniency of rules gives us all more freedom to be comfortable at work; however, it also leaves the onus on us to decide what is appropriate and what is crossing the line. When in doubt, it is probably useful to look to the executives of the company to set the tone. By following their lead, you are sure not to make a risky choice.

Creating a Dependable Wardrobe

Today's lifestyle can encompass a variety of events within a single day—going to the gym, office, dinner with a client. Since it's unlikely that you'll have time for a quick wardrobe change, buying and wearing clothes that work within a variety of scenarios will make these transitions easier.

Following is a shopping list recommended by Banana Republic's Christina Gabriel. But keep in mind, these are general suggestions. Add your own style and flair to this basic wardrobe.

Every modern woman should have:

High-quality suit

Skirt that works in with the suit

Layering blouses

Cashmere twin-set

Versatile pants

Tweed pants

Sweater of the season

The great black dress

Quality leather handbag

Novelty fun bags

A great pair of boots

Strappy black shoes

Accessory of the season

Every modern man should have:

A good-quality suit

Woven shirt

Button-down shirt

Range of ties

Khakis

Pants of the season

A leather briefcase

Oxford shoes

Loafers

Great leather jacket

Versatile sweater

Religious Services

Just as a casual office has become commonplace, the dress-down approach has infiltrated its way into the most sacred places. I've been known to wear tennis clothes and shorts at my church during the summer months, but, once having spotted a woman wearing a bathing suit and an almost see-through dress, I was reformed. Never again would I wear shorts to church despite what the rest of the congregation deems appropriate. Who doesn't admire a woman dressed in an elegant linen dress accessorized with such understated touches as a chic hat or simple strand of pearls? And the men in their blue blazers, bright ties, and loafers? After all, they are dressing for a higher authority.

According to the book of modern Jewish etiquette, in the traditional view, one is expected to reserve one's finest garments and ornaments for wear on the Sabbath and holidays. A well-tailored pantsuit for women or a sports jacket in more quiet tones for men might meet this standard. When in doubt, one should lean to the fashionable suit or more conservative attire—pantsuits, however, would never be acceptable in an Orthodox synagogue, and married women must always wear hats or other headcoverings.

Funerals

Conservative attire is always best. Wearing all black is so past century, but bright colors are garish. Funerals are not the best venue to make any fashion statements, and controversial attire should be saved for that wild party.

Holidays

I'm going to sound like your old aunt Peg on this one. Holidays happen a few times a year. When it's a family occasion celebrating a meaningful event, it won't kill you to wear something nice. Dressing up is traditional and keeps the season festive. However, the dress code for such occasions is ultimately up to each family.

Weddings

First and foremost, there's only one woman at a wedding who should be wearing a white dress. After that basic rule, follow the invitation. Weddings before 6:00 P.M. are not usually black tie unless specified. However, this doesn't mean that you should wear your office attire. Women have a daunting array of options—there are cocktail dresses, pantsuits, skirts, and gowns. A wedding is the best venue to dress up in your favorite fashions—add some flair with a sophisticated hat or vintage dress. The guys tend to always go with their standard khakis and blue blazer combo. Sometimes a crisp pin-striped suit with a festive tie separates the well-dressed from the men who look as if they're attending a semiformal at the frat house.

When Christiane Lemieux and Josh Young were married—a laid-back couple who appreciate an equally laid-back lifestyle—family and friends were surprised that their wedding called for black tie. "Everyone looked fantastic," says Lemieux. "And the guests were pleasantly surprised by how fun it was to dress up. While women typically enjoy making the effort, some of the younger men tend to feel uncomfortable in a tux." Many men look to dressing in a tuxedo as uncreative, like connecting the dots. Says Lemieux, "There's little self-expression, or it's too formal and stuffy. So many of the men personalized their tuxes with a tie as opposed to a bow. My husband wore a silver tie with his tux and looked really hip."

What's Black Tie?

Sometimes when I go to a formal event, I am surprised to see so many women in their nightgowns. Ah, the young, social, stylish set—but do they look beautiful? Not always. Such evening wear leaves absolutely nothing to the imagination. However, are the veteran grand dames, cloaked in their poofy ball gowns and glitzy handbags, the model? Hardly. An evening look should be understated and elegant—this is where the simple approach is an approach worth taking. As understated as a long sheath dress created from French satin with a delicate choker, matching handbag, and wrap. And what man doesn't look his best in a classic tux?

Since finding an evening dress is as challenging as shopping for a bathing suit, investing in one good dress is always a safe approach. It's not as if you are going to the Golden Globes one month and then being analyzed by the fashion experts at the Oscars the next. It's fine to wear the dress many times over. Just change the accessories.

> ## Past Century/ Present Century
>
> *If you are suddenly hit by a fit of sneezes, it's doubtful and unnecessary that the man next to you will offer you his handkerchief. Obviously the idea of a shared handkerchief is unsanitary, unhealthy, and—not to mention—gross.*

DO'S

1. Do take time to find cuts and styles that fit your proportions.
2. Do buy more than one item in different colors if it fits well.
3. Do dress in a style similar to your prospective employers on a job interview.
4. Do notice the difference of office attire for different industries.
5. Do make the effort to dress on holiday occasions.

DON'TS

① Don't blindly follow fashion trends.

② Don't shop alone if you are uncertain about your taste in clothing.

③ Don't mistake professional clothing for being well-dressed.

④ Don't dress in casual attire when attending a religious service.

⑤ Don't overaccessorize when attending a black-tie affair.

DRESS CODE QUIZ

In developing your personal style, it is important to:
 A. Feel confident.
 B. Understand your body type.
 C. Know how clothes flatter you.
 D. All of the above.

ANSWER: D

You should dress for work:
 A. In the most conservative attire you own.
 B. In a look that complements the company's image.
 C. In whatever makes you comfortable.
 D. Men should wear a jacket and tie, and ladies a dress or pantsuit.

ANSWER: B

When building a wardrobe, it's important to consider clothes that:
 A. Work within different settings.
 B. Are inexpensive.
 C. Are trendy.
 D. Will last a long time.

ANSWER: A

Every man's wardrobe should have:
 A. A pant of the season.
 B. A pair of khakis.
 C. A suit.
 D. All of the above.

ANSWER: D

According to modern Jewish etiquette, on the Sabbath and holidays, you should wear:

    A. All black.

    B. Your finest garments and ornaments.

    C. Hats.

    D. Anything but jeans.

ANSWER: B

For weddings after 6:00 P.M., you should wear:

    A. Anything festive.

    B. Professional clothes.

    C. Formal attire.

    D. Any of the above.

ANSWER: C

Expert Advice

Kate Spade, Designer

Fashionably Appropriate

Kate Spade is not only the internationally recognized designer known for her one-of-a-kind accessories, she is also beautifully mannered—skilled in the classic art of etiquette that one would expect of a lady carrying a Kate Spade bag. Employees that come to work for her company share her etiquette ethic—it's even written in the employee handbook, advocating a "clean, polite atmosphere."

Tradition begins in childhood. My favorite fashion memories are when my mother dressed me in my shiny black-patent leathers and a party dress, saved for the most festive occasions.

When my husband, Andy, and I moved to New York over a decade ago, one of our fondest memories was having lunch at the Plaza. I will never forget the taste of the tuna sandwich on lightly toasted white bread, garnishes of parsley, and a pickle speared with an elaborately topped toothpick. Andy wore his best navy blazer and I wore a camel cashmere cable-knit sweater, a houndstooth jacket, and charcoal flannel cigarette pants. One of the things that made this lunch special and memorable was the fact that we'd purposely dressed to have an elegant lunch at the Plaza.

Andy and I recently rekindled our lunch at the Plaza and were disappointed to discover that the "jacket required" sign is no longer posted. Youths wearing tourist sweatshirts and baseball hats now sat in a dramatic contrast to the vaulted ceilings decorated with crystal chandeliers and tables scented with exotic flowers. To use an antiquated term relating to my antiquated memories, am I *square*? Is my desire to dress appropriately for formal occasions as dated as a Lime Ricky?

Fashion has been experiencing a new form of leniency; Andy and I bemoan this subject endlessly. Not only do we enjoy such rare treats as a formal affair, lavish dinner, or the theater—it's the preparing for that event that especially marks the occasion. The right shoes, jewelry, and, to no surprise, a handbag, rekindles that childhood excitement of black patents and a pretty dress. I recently experienced similar remorse when we went to the ballet, though my festive attire was most suitable to watch a prima ballerina pirouette, I was overly dressed in a theater filled with patrons in casual attire. Like the elegant decor of the Plaza, the splendor of a theater deserves an audience with attire to match—and I've always been one for matching.

A feeling of renewed spirit and optimism came with the new century, and there are new accessories that came along with it. As the world hastily navigates a futuristic course, fashion has embraced the return of sophistication. Celebrating and dressing up is the trend of the moment, and it has my vote to stay in style. Farewell to grunge, with a nod to elegance. Time to make another reservation at the Plaza!

CHAPTER

PROPRIETY
IN THE
WORKPLACE

*T*he great thing about working in a professional environment is that there is typically no room for cattiness. Not that cattiness is completely foreign to corporate culture—as anyone in the fashion and entertainment industry can attest to—but there is a general understanding as to appropriate business decorum, which allows work to be done efficiently and fellow employees to perform their jobs to the best of their ability. No matter how successful a person may become in his or her career, it is essential to remember that courtesy comes first, even in the workplace. The ability to work with others is always a sterling asset. From the mailroom to the CEO, every person in a company needs to uphold office etiquette— their job may be depending on it.

The Job Interview

A good job interview is a mutual collaboration between interviewer and interviewee: a learning process, as much for the applicant as for the employer. The interviewee should come prepared with a polished résumé, an understanding about the job for which he is applying, and a list of questions that he may want to address. (See also Chapter XIII, "Dress Code," on dressing for the job interview.)

I've always believed that the one giving the interview should begin with a description of the company, the position available, and any benefits the company can offer to the candidate. By learning the benefits in the beginning, the candidate isn't left in the awkward position of having to ask about the added benefits.

However, if the prospective employer does not mention benefits in the beginning of the interview, the candidate should wait until all other questions relating to the job have been asked and answered before finally asking about benefits and vacation. These are legitimate questions, but keep in mind the interviewer is gauging your experience and enthusiasm for the work ahead, not on how well you can perform on a vacation day.

The candidate should keep answers focused and to the point. Refrain from turning the tables and asking the employer about her accomplishments and professional history, which will only appear presumptuous.

At the interview's close, thank the person for her time and wait to hear how she will be in touch. Send a thank-you note so you will stand out if there are several applicants for the same job and, moreover, to fur-

ther express your interest in the job. Try to mention specifics of the conversation, to fix the interview permanently in the interviewer's mind, and try to send the letter the same day, before the hiring decision is made. If you have not heard back from the interviewer in the time that she said she would get back to you, it's permissible to make a follow-up call. Sometimes filling a position takes time—issues from office space to budget can all factor into a delayed response. (See Chapter X, "Family Matters," for teens on a job interview.)

General Office Decorum

A personable coworker is always a pleasure to be around. I had one person who worked for me who didn't have it in her nature to smile. This always seemed to create a rather dour working environment. At the New York Presbyterian Hospital, where I am the vice chairman, one of the key things we stress to our employees is that they try to smile as often as possible. It's so much easier than having to explain why you are in a bad mood. The security guard, doorman, and receptionist are always so upbeat, which is especially important in a hospital environment when many visitors are in a somber mood. My spirits are always uplifted by the doorman at the hospital, who always greets me with a genuine: "Good morning, it's nine-thirty-five A.M., have a pleasant day."

How to Be Boss-y

The hardest job of a boss may not be bringing in more clients or managing the bottom line, but rather keeping the people who work for you happy. A leader who earns the support and respect of her employees will get back a happier, more productive workforce in return—and *that* makes managing the bottom line even easier.

Good managers in business guarantee the productivity of the office. They are responsible for their employees' welfare and satisfaction. They know how to delegate responsibility and feel secure in doing so. Earning a leadership role doesn't entitle you to an "I'm the boss!" attitude, which can only be met with a lack of respect from others. Those who work under you can hear only so many times that you graduated from Harvard Business School before they'll want to tell you where to put your diploma.

Many times people in executive and administrative positions realize that they don't know or can't do everything that must be done. A smart, successful boss will use her power wisely and have the confidence to hire good people who, in turn, will keep the manager looking good.

Diplomacy and tact are also key attributes for those in command. It is important to listen carefully to basic questions addressed by less experienced employees and to answer such questions clearly, patiently, and thoroughly at the opportune moment.

Respect for others and a sense of humor is also key to good management. Any manager can become a better manager if he doesn't always take himself so seriously and is generally responsive to workers' needs.

The Office Peon

"I went to school for this?" A typical mantra that young, ambitious professionals intone when beginning at the bottom of the totem pole. Don't be surprised if after three rounds of interviews, acing your entrance test, and securing a job that over thirty other applicants were in the running for, your prime function turns out to be faxing internationally. The expression "paying your dues" may sound like a more suitable option, since any payment out of this seemingly humiliating role is the better alternative.

However, a talented person who is confident that he can contribute more should keep in mind that his new company may want to take some time with him—slowly cultivating responsibilities. An employer's rational is to learn how the support staff can do just that—support the staff. As minor as lowly tasks may seem, they need to be mastered. Just one abrupt phone call or lost message from a client, and the results could be disastrous for the company. Entry-level employees demonstrate their capabilities on the little things (so don't give your manager a latte when he asked for an espresso!). Once the employer has confidence in you, added responsibilities will be forthcoming. If, after a reasonable period, such opportunities are not forthcoming, make an appointment with your supervisor to outline your strengths, weaknesses, and projected goals and growth within the company.

At the opposite end of the spectrum are entry-level employees who, due to lack of staff or a high-pressure environment, may feel overwhelmed, like they've been thrown into the ocean at high tide without knowing how to swim. Keep in mind that you were probably hired because the manager felt that you had the survival skills to stay afloat. This kind of environment is best suited for the quick learner, who can pick up from her surroundings without being a burden to those around her. While it is true that "no question is a dumb question," the approach is important. Be practical—use common sense. Be sensitive to the fact that your boss's time is limited. Asking your manager how to write a sales pitch two hours before a company presentation isn't convenient for anyone. Conversely, if your boss wants something delivered to a client that you spent the entire day feverishly producing, don't wait until the next morning to ask if it should be sent via overnight or regular mail.

Getting Coffee

The stigma of the steno-writing secretary who fetches coffee for her boss is rather past century. If I were seated next to an office mate who took a quick break from his desk, only to return with a hot cup in his hand from the café across the block, I'd find it a tad selfish that he didn't ask me if I would like anything.

Past Century/ Present Century

Ordering flowers, attending to the boss's dry cleaning, and fetching coffee was once the role of the female secretary supporting the professional man's every need. Now the high-powered woman executive can order in coffee for herself.

Don't be fooled into thinking that making a coffee run is a duty for those of lesser rank. It's just being considerate, which is what manners are all about. If one person is ordering lunch in, for example, what's the harm in asking those around you if they to would like to split an order? This is practical, not punishment.

Under Pressure

"I'll only know how capable he'll be when placed in a stressful situation," said a friend to me recently in regards to a new business associate. This is what distinguishes a warrior from a worker. Another friend of mine learned a valuable, career-long lesson at her first job from the COO of a major company. Trying to meet a delivery deadline, assistants scrambled under the duress of panic. Filling out last-minute forms, checking to see that the contact information was correct—in this late hour, the COO remained late, working with employees on every level, to ensure that the project was being effectively handled. In the midst of the last-minute chaos, the phone interrupted everyone's frenzy. While the crew decided to just ignore the setback of a late-night call, the COO picked up the phone with the calmness of a yoga instructor. He then proceeded to help the caller, graciously, in fact, even transferring the caller to the appropriate line. Playing the role of an assistant, he had no pretense of position. This leader reacted with a coolness and efficiency that easily earns him a lofty role.

When the pressure is turned on, don't let it show. Showing the stress doesn't get the job done any faster or better. Create a more pleasant atmosphere, and the work always gets done.

Encouraging Words

If someone does a good job, she'd be crazy not to want to hear it. Consider how you feel when someone takes you aside to tell you what a solid effort you did on your latest project. No matter what rank, from the CEO who just did a bang-up job appearing on CNBC to the person in the mailroom who stayed late in order to send an urgent package, one word of praise can mean quite a lot. When deserved, these sentiments can carry the positive momentum toward the next challenge.

Working with Your Assistant

It's been said that type A people hire type A people. However, it's not always a good idea to hire an ambitious secretary—unless you want a short-term employee or someone who is devising machinations for your job that will make the House of Medici seem like play school.

Whom you hire should depend primarily on the type of work that you need done. If you have a lot of clerical work and there is little chance of growth, appoint someone who is satisfied with this role. If, however, you're poised for a promotion and you want to groom someone for your position, then look for a candidate who will be able to step up. To avoid an assistant's constant nipping at your toes, you can address unnecessary subterfuge during an interview—clearly outlining the job, what is expected, and what is intolerable. You can also detect during an interview if you have good working chemistry—the key to any positive relationship. Once the assistant is hired, mistakes will naturally be made. One learns by doing, and this curve should be understood. Both the boss and assistant need to be sensitive to this. In order to correct the mistake, collect your thoughts and calmly ask to speak to your assistant in private. You might say: "I wish this hadn't happened. How can we avoid the problem in the future?" Then you can both work through it together, avoiding any similar situations from occurring in the future.

Your assistant is the one person in the office whom you depend on regularly. Therefore, you should always show your mutual respect for each other. An assistant should make her boss look good, and the boss should hold his assistant in high regard in front of others.

Office Mentor

Anyone who takes their career seriously should always have an office mentor, that "go-to" person who can advise you on everything from how to handle the prickly client to improving your chances for advancement within the company. The mentor you choose should be well respected, have worked in the company for some time, and show the willingness to advise and nurture. Invest the time in the relationship that it takes to develop the chemistry, prove your value, and demonstrate your loyalty.

Keeping Someone Waiting

When you have to keep someone waiting, send your assistant to apologize for you and to give a reason for your delay. The assistant should offer the person waiting something to drink or a magazine. If you'll be tied up for more than fifteen minutes or so, it's best to make an appearance and apologize in person. Ask the person waiting if it wouldn't be more convenient if he could come back later or reschedule for a less hectic day.

Office Complaints

If you have a sensitive problem at the office, possibly with another colleague, budget discrepancy, etc., it is best to speak with your supervisor first, and discuss the situation. Afterward, you should document the conversation in writing with a memo stating what took place during the discussion and what you understand will be the steps taken to remedy the situation. Be careful, however, that you don't inundate your boss with weekly problems—choose your dilemmas wisely.

Discussing Salary in the Workplace

Discussing your salary is gauche. In the workplace, it's simply senseless. Salaries are often set based on negotiation and circumstance. An employer may give one worker a higher salary over another with a similar job description because that person may have more to offer the company in terms of contacts, potential clients, experience, etc. To discuss your salary with fellow workers can only promote ill will between colleagues and/or employees and employers.

Personal Life in a Professional Environment

The very word "personal" relates to situations of a private nature, directly opposite of professional. Thus mixing personal with professional can be an ill-fated combination. It's only natural to include pictures of your family and friends on your desk, or to share personal stories with office mates, but take it further by discussing problems or, perhaps, a new relationship and your professional demeanor may begin to wane. Giving a coworker personal insight could expose a vulnerable side to your character while also making him or her feel uncomfortable being privy to such information. Inversely, sharing problems of a certain nature with your boss may lead him or her to wonder if you are capable of doing your job. However, if you are going through a difficult period that is guaranteed to affect your job performance, you may choose to share this information with your boss or colleagues along with a specific time when you predict the problem will no longer be a hindrance.

Sexual Harassment

Chasing secretaries around the boardroom table is so circa 1957 advertising executive. Giving compliments and then being sued is so Supreme Court Hearings, circa 1992. Yet, now that more men and women are dating in the workplace, how does one negotiate asking a colleague out without having a lawsuit thrown at one?

If a coworker makes a sexual advance, and that attraction is not reciprocated, it needs to end there. By saying simply, "I have and can only consider our relationship on a professional basis," he or she will hopefully end any further pursuit. The moments after the advance will undoubtedly be uncomfortable for all parties. Maintaining your professional responsibilities and focusing on the work that needs to be done together could alleviate some of the tension.

In layman's terms, sexual harassment is when there is unwelcome sexual advances, requests for sexual favors, or any abuse of a sexual nature. It is illegal, and an employee has rights, no matter how junior her position. Victims of sexual harassment should speak to their supervisor or human resources department. They will most likely ask you to record the specific incidents, even documenting precise times and dates.

A boss should never ask his or her assistant out. If the assistant is attracted to his supervisor, and the supervisor seems to share this affection, they should begin the relationship cautiously. Complications involving all professional contacts should be considered.

At Home at Work

It takes a laptop, fax machine, and e-mail, and then, suddenly, you're in business. "In the globally connected world that we live in today," says Nancy Cherner, an asset manager who works from her Manhattan apartment, "you can be connected to businesses from just about anywhere—all you need is the tools." The perks: Your commute is short, there are no office politics, and forget casual Fridays when you can wear your pajamas.

With all of the added bonuses, you need to also be aware of how to operate your business so that you're not inclined to constantly raid the fridge and become more conversant with the daytime soap scandal than your work schedule. Discipline is key. The hardest adjustment may be to the lack of structure. You are suddenly faced with overwhelming freedom, which can be confusing. Questions will arise, such as, When do you begin your day and when should it end? How can you organize your business tools in your private home? Can a private and professional life exist together under one roof? Before beginning an at-home office, consider your traits. Cherner says that folks who are disciplined, entrepreneurial, and self-motivated are good candidates for self-employment.

To maintain a professional mind in a personal space, consider regulating standard business hours—especially if your work contacts are operating under the same schedule. If a contact calls you at 9:30 A.M., for example, and it sounds like he just woke you up, that does not project the right image. The sound of your microwave popcorn being made, barking dogs, and the *The Price Is Right* reruns are also not conducive to a professional impression. Conversely, some home offices do not have a dedicated business line. Business contacts should respect that by calling only at reasonable workday hours. "I was really annoyed when I received a call from an editor after nine-thirty P.M.," a freelance writer once told me.

If you're able, make the investment to equip your home office with all of your professional needs so you can function as efficiently as possible. Designate a specific area in your home as the "work area" so that you can unwind and enjoy your home without having to feel threatened by impending deadlines 24/7.

Cherner not only lives in a residential area that's on the edge of Manhattan's midtown, which "psychologically puts you in the game" and is convenient for meetings with nearby firms, but she also has the technology tools that she needs. "I am hyperconnected to the outside world and also very technology-oriented."

Christmas Presents

As Christmas has lost its yuletide merriment with the mad rush to get everyone from your personal trainer to your child's kindergarten teacher a thoughtful gift, office presents should be given to the one or two employees with whom you share a close relationship. Something personal and fairly inexpensive is a traditional gesture. This can be a scented candle, book, or CD. Beauty items and gourmet treats are also good ideas.

An executive who has had the same assistant for years may want to give her a more expensive gift. However, this could be awkward for the assistant, since it is obvious that she cannot match the dollar amount of such a gift. A clever present that you know she will appreciate is a more suitable gesture.

In some instances bigger corporations give a standard gift to their employees. Even if you have no use for a bath towel with the company logo, no one can help but feel warmed by a present. After all, isn't it the thought that counts, no matter how mass-produced it is?

When You Receive an Unexpected Gift

Quash the temptation to run out during your lunch hour and stress shop to reciprocate the unexpected gift. Instead, thank the giver and tell him or her how much you like your gift.

Business Functions

No, a work-related social event is not the right time to tell that guy in accounting that you secretly lust for him. I know of one national men's magazine that has an annual Christmas party policy that states that any actions or behavior at the office celebration will be forgotten the next day. But when the guy in ad sales treats everyone to a private viewing of his boxer shorts printed with tiny candy canes, it takes quite a memory to forget.

Instead, it's wise to try to disengage yourself from any inappropriate advances or conversations at such functions. Also, if you don't want to wake up the next morning thinking "I wish I'd never done that," it's im-

portant for you to know your alcohol limits. Feel free to enjoy the more relaxed social atmosphere, just don't let it get out of control.

For those of you thinking of opting out, think again. It's advisable to attend any business function that is evaluated as important to the company. For the regular business events to appease clients, you can be a bit more selective. For the annual company picnic and Christmas party, you need to make the effort. Great planning went into the function. It is also an opportunity to socialize with colleagues and help improve office relations.

Mingling

Some of us would rather get our teeth cleaned than circulate at a party. Just add a professional responsibility to the social function, and, suddenly, you're wishing for root canal. Cocktail chatter is a skill. Some people are so good, they could get a British Beefeater to chuckle, while others would rather hide out in the rest rooms until the entire affair is over.

The best way to mingle is to just feel comfortable and confident. Wear your favorite clothes or make a date to attend the function with your favorite office mate, anything that puts you in the right mood.

At a business party, the people you behave with professionally, from the mailroom worker to the CEO, suddenly become your social partners. Business becomes pleasure. This is a welcomed opportunity to cross boundaries. An opportunity to talk to those in the company who are higher ranked than you. If you find yourself next to the company's chairman whom you've never met, introduce yourself and keep the conversation fairly short. You shouldn't be too intimidated, since the company leader probably has some skill in leading such conversations along.

All out of clever witticisms? Don't fret, as I am sure that you have volumes of work-related topics to discuss. However, don't spread gossip and don't say anything catty—you never know what can come back to haunt you.

If you're unsure of what territory to cover, without getting too personal, some safe questions are:

- What are you doing for the holidays?
- Where is your family from?
- Any good movies out right now?
- Wasn't that a funny e-mail about buying raffle tickets the chairman sent the other day?

Handing Business Cards

One savvy friend of mine always keeps a stack of business cards in his left pocket and puts the ones that he receives in his right pocket. This takes out all of the awkward exchanges, sifting through your endless bag in search of a dog-eared card.

Exiting Gracefully

Those who have the bad taste to leave a company with the braggadocio of a sailor about to charter the world may only find themselves washed up after the first storm. Failed performances at a new position are most certainly a consideration when leaving a job. But, career security aside, it's only proper to leave a company with the dignity and respect that are associated with consummate professionalism. Industries are small, and your reputation is as good as a former colleague's word. It's not uncommon that someone you worked with in a past job will eventually work with you

Past Century/ Present Century

The wife of a successful businessman who attended many social functions was often expected to accompany her husband. Conversely, a husband with an executive wife with similar demands was not necessarily expected to accompany her. Today, however, busy wives may bow out with valid excuses. Whomever the invitation was issued to should be responsible for answering it.

again in a future one. Keep your relations dignified both during and after you work at a company. It will serve you best in the long run.

DO'S

❶ Do uphold office etiquette.

❷ Do keep in good spirits in a professional environment.

❸ Do use a little psychology in your professional dealings with others.

❹ Do keep regular business hours in a home office.

❺ Do exit a company on good terms.

DON'TS

① Don't interview the person giving an interview.

② Don't ask your boss a frivolous question at an inconvenient time.

③ Don't make a coffee run without asking others if they would like some, too.

④ Don't keep someone waiting for more than fifteen minutes without an explanation.

⑤ Don't fraternize in the office.

PROPRIETY IN THE WORKPLACE QUIZ

When interviewing a candidate for employment, you should begin by:
- A. Allowing the candidate to go over his qualifications.
- B. Describing the company, position, and any perks.
- C. Asking the candidate relevant questions.
- D. Introducing the candidate to fellow employees.

ANSWER: B

If you have not heard from the company that interviewed you after a few weeks, it's appropriate to:
- A. Make a follow-up call.
- B. Assume that the position has been filled.
- C. Be patient.
- D. Any of the above.

ANSWER: A

The best managers:
- A. Are drill sergeants.
- B. Are feared by those who work beneath them.
- C. Have good contacts.
- D. Feel secure in their own position.

ANSWER: D

If a newly hired entry-level employee feels she is not being fully uti-lized, she should:
- A. Complain to senior management.
- B. Make an appointment with human resources.
- C. Look for another job.
- D. Be patient and work as hard as she can with her given re-sponsibilities.

ANSWER: D

A senior-level employee should never:
- A. Answer his own phone.
- B. Go to the mailroom.
- C. Feel it beneath him to perform administrative tasks.
- D. Help his assistant.

ANSWER: C

If someone you work with makes a sexual advance that you do not want to reciprocate, initially you should:
- A. File for sexual harassment.
- B. Speak to your human resources director.
- C. Ask to be transferred.
- D. Tell him that you only look to him professionally.

ANSWER: D

Christmas presents should be given to:
- A. Everyone at the office.
- B. One or two of your closest colleagues.
- C. Your supervisor.
- D. The mailroom workers.

ANSWER: B

The best place to socialize with the company chairman is:
- A. At an office party.
- B. Before a board meeting.
- C. On the elevator.
- D. Any of the above.

ANSWER: A

CHAPTER

FINANCIAL MANNERS

$\mathcal{I}$s money the root of all evil, or is greed good? It's an endless debate, but no one can deny that financial issues have the ability to cause both social faux pas and irreparable disagreements. As one needs self-control with alcohol, work, stress—self-control when it comes to monetary manners is as much a consideration.

One major "Don't" with regard to money is to talk about how much you have. It's gauche and makes other people feel uncomfortable. When meeting with friends or acquaintances, the genuine ones are more interested in spending some time with their friends, exchanging in an enlightening conversation, and, most likely, have little interest in discussing the monthly statements of someone's bank account.

Spending Wisely

Whoever designed currency should have added a warning label: Caution—abuse of this product can cause financial ruin, tasteless behavior, and extreme pomposity. Spending lavishly on chi-chi dinners, flashy cars, and extravagant trips sounds exciting, but in reality, it's more like a sip of espresso—giving you a quick jolt but hardly the energy needed to sustain an active day. There's a way to spend that will merit its rightful appreciation from the consumer, showing a sense of worth, and then there's buying haphazardly only because you can.

I know of one woman who is beautiful, sophisticated, and sweet—too nice to hate! I've always admired her for never using her financial status as a draw. She could live over her means but chooses to be more frugal.

If you do come into some into money, it's a good time to find out what gives you purpose and motivation. Always continue to do the projects and roles that provide fulfillment rather than dramatically change to a life that you may not have any preparation for.

Friends Suddenly Coming into Money

Most of us spend time with others who share our common interests and make us feel happy. However, when one friend reaches a certain financial level, inevitably, that friend will become acquainted with new people. It can become difficult and awkward to maintain a friendship when a financial imbalance evolves—an old friend may not be able to afford your new lifestyle. Remember, though, solid relations take time to build and are based on loyalty and an understanding of each other. For those who come into money suddenly, they need to be more aware of who is entering their life and why. Be wary of the people who are lobbying extremely hard to become your new best friend. Don't be surprised if suddenly they ask you for "just a small favor."

Living Beyond Your Means

I've always found people who live beyond their means to be lost individuals. Images of fame, wealth, and affluence that are continually glamorized in the media becomes a superficial standard some try to uphold. While it is most likely impossible to achieve the kind of fortunes fit for a rock star, security in the comforts one works for should be enough to be proud of. A person who buys things frivolously for the sake of image tells me that she is pretending to be something that she is not. It's a shame that she cannot be comfortable with who she is. Again, genuine people—people of worth and respect—do not evaluate others by material possessions.

Living beyond your means, on a pragmatic level, makes financial security difficult to attain. It only sets the path for future financial difficulties—a leading cause of hardship and relationship rifts.

Friends and Money

If you are in a position where you and a friend have to deal with money matters, perhaps because you are going on a trip together or sharing a rental, it's best to get it in writing. Even though this may be awkward since you are friends, it's less awkward than having to make sense of any financial misunderstandings.

Asking someone for money

If you are in need of money, just be honest and ask. You should ask relations before friends. For example, just say, "I am unable to pay for John's tuition this semester, could I ask for a loan?" All transactions need to be outlined in a written statement that establishes the date by which you will be paid back and whether or not any interest will be incurred.

How to handle someone who asks you for money

Honesty is best here as well. If you can't assist in that person's request, just say, "At this time I'm not in the position to do that."

How to ask for money owed to you

How wonderful it would be if you received money back before you even noticed that a debt had not been paid. If you are in a position where the person to whom you had loaned money has not paid you back and you feel it is too awkward a thing to ask, one option is to blame your accountant by saying, "My bookkeeper has been pestering me about not having received the money I loaned to you." Or, another option is to kindly re-mind the person, "Do you have my address so you know where to mail the check?" After that, make a promise to yourself regarding whom you can and cannot lend money to in the future.

Trading Stocks

If you bought a stock on the low and sold it on the high, you are either ex-tremely lucky or lying. And everyone knows that it is not polite to lie. When discussing your personal portfolio, it is boastful to disclose your big wins without discussing your losses.

Monetary issues and friends don't always mix; it's best not to make stock recommendations to personal relations—even if it does make you a lot of money, it can just as easily lose you money and possibly lose you a friend. If the recommendation doesn't pan out, you can't help but feel responsible, and, possibly, your friend may become resentful. And, as with all monetary is-sues, never discuss an exact dollar amount of your personal portfolio.

Tipping

When an airport carrier assists with your bag or a service truck gives your car a jump, they are not just doing it because they are being nice—it's their job. Tips are how many people earn a living. Being aware of who deserves a tip is really more of a responsibility than a good deed.

The standard amount for most mandatory tips is 15 to 20 percent, depending on the service and your satisfaction. For those who never excelled at percentages back in grade school days, just find out what 10 percent of the total sum is and then add from there. For example, 10 percent of ten dollars is one dollar, 20 percent is two dollars. Also, it's perfectly acceptable to round up to the next highest dollar.

You could also carry around with you this handy tip chart that conveniently fits into a wallet for more complicated bills.

Check	15%	20%	Check	15%	20%	Check	15%	20%
10.00	$1.50	$2.00	41.00	6.15	8.20	72.00	10.80	14.40
11.00	1.65	2.20	42.00	6.30	8.40	73.00	10.95	14.60
12.00	1.80	2.40	43.00	6.45	8.60	74.00	11.10	14.80
13.00	1.95	2.60	44.00	6.60	8.80	75.00	11.25	15.00
14.00	2.10	2.80	45.00	6.75	9.00	76.00	11.40	15.20
15.00	2.25	3.00	46.00	6.90	9.20	77.00	11.55	15.40
16.00	2.40	3.20	47.00	7.05	9.40	78.00	11.70	15.60
17.00	2.55	3.40	48.00	7.20	9.60	79.00	11.85	15.80
18.00	2.70	3.60	49.00	7.35	9.80	80.00	12.00	16.00
19.00	2.85	3.80	50.00	7.50	10.00	81.00	12.15	16.20
20.00	3.00	4.00	51.00	7.65	10.20	82.00	12.30	16.40
21.00	3.15	4.20	52.00	7.80	10.40	83.00	12.45	16.60
22.00	3.30	4.40	53.00	7.95	10.60	84.00	12.60	16.80
23.00	3.45	4.60	54.00	8.10	10.80	85.00	12.75	17.00
24.00	3.60	4.80	55.00	8.25	11.00	86.00	12.90	17.20
25.00	3.75	5.00	56.00	8.40	11.20	87.00	13.05	17.40
26.00	3.90	5.20	57.00	8.55	11.40	88.00	13.20	17.60
27.00	4.05	5.40	58.00	8.70	11.60	89.00	13.35	16.80
28.00	4.20	5.60	59.00	8.85	11.80	90.00	13.50	18.00
29.00	4.35	5.80	60.00	9.00	12.00	91.00	13.65	18.20
30.00	4.50	6.00	61.00	9.15	12.20	92.00	13.80	18.40
31.00	4.65	6.20	62.00	9.30	12.40	93.00	13.95	18.60
32.00	4.80	6.40	63.00	9.45	12.60	94.00	14.10	18.80
33.00	4.95	6.60	64.00	9.60	12.80	95.00	14.25	19.00
34.00	5.10	6.80	65.00	9.75	13.00	96.00	14.40	19.20
35.00	5.25	7.00	66.00	9.90	13.20	97.00	14.55	19.40
36.00	5.40	7.20	67.00	10.05	13.40	98.00	14.70	19.60
37.00	5.55	7.40	68.00	10.20	13.60	99.00	14.85	19.80
38.00	5.70	7.60	69.00	10.35	13.80	100.00	15.00	20.00
39.00	5.85	7.80	70.00	10.50	14.00			
40.00	6.00	8.00	71.00	10.65	14.20			

The following is a list of general recommendations for tipping:

Restaurants

(See Chapter IV, "Dining Right.")

Bars

The bartender should be tipped 15 to 20 percent of your drink.

Caterers

The caterer is paid the rate that you have established, but his employees should be tipped. Ask your caterer the standard amount, as the amount varies throughout parts of the country.

Salons

Keep in mind that most workers in a salon—including the hair washer, colorist, and coat check person—usually depend on tips. For hair colorists who usually spend two hours with me, 20 percent of the bill is appropriate assuming I'm satisfied with their service. A safe amount for a masseuse, manicurist, facialist, and other beauty services is 15 to 20 percent. Before you go in for your appointment, clear the tip amount with the receptionist, since salons' tip rates may vary.

At Yves Duref's eponymous salon in Manhattan, if Yves cuts your hair, he won't accept a tip since his "name is on the window."

Suggests Yves, if you're really satisfied, 20 percent is a nice tip. The hair washer gets 10 percent, 10 percent for the colorist—the lowest person makes the lowest money.

Yves also recommends that you tip the employees in person—since they are so busy, they sometimes forget who gave them what. A sensible approach that some of Yves's clients take is to have the tips already prepared in envelopes with the attendants' names on them. And, says Yves in his humble French accent, "it really is more about the appreciation than the money."

Rest room attendants

If there is a rest room attendant, she is usually there to assist you with a towel or some of the beauty products that are available. She expects to be tipped for this service. If you do not have any change on you (typically one dollar), then do not use any of the toiletries, politely smile, and apologize for not having your wallet with you.

Apartments

I give the workers in my apartment building a monthly fee for tips so I don't have to always reach for my purse. If you're just out of school, a young couple starting out, or anyone who has budgetary constraints, a small tip is understandable. Otherwise home-baked goods with a thoughtful note is a generous gesture.

Food deliveries

Considering that the guy who delivers your pizza can have as dangerous a job as a police officer or fireman, tipping him is the right thing to do. A tip of 10 percent is fair. If the bill comes to less than two dollars, that should be the standard minimum tip.

Many delivery people pay for their own gas and use their own transportation. And, for the delivery person who walked up four flights of stairs so you can conveniently have your wonton soup, tip him extra!

Taxis

New York City cab drivers expect 20 percent of the fare. If your cab driver has chosen an out-of-way route mistaking you for a tourist, I don't think he deserves a tip at all.

Also, I can only guess how many umbrellas and gloves the New York City Taxi and Limousine Service has of mine. While it's important to have your belongings ready so you can exit the cab promptly, don't let the driver rush you out. Your safety and comfort are the priority. I like to put my change safely back in my wallet rather than have to attend to loose bills outside of the cab. Take your time and assure your driver by saying, "Just a moment, please, while I gather my things."

Caddies

Caddies are usually tipped after the eighteenth hole, and all players should be prepared to tip them. If you're a guest at someone's private club, pay the greens fee and your caddie's fee, unless you are also a member of the golf course, in which case you need only repay your host. At a club where members are billed later for the greens fee, a guest pays both caddies' fees. If, in either case, your host makes a point of stopping you, it is your duty to stand firm and pay.

Car service/tow trucks

Even if you have a pre-established car service with your vehicle, or are a member of AAA, if the service truck staff takes care of you and does a good job, he should be rewarded with a tip. This could be five dollars, or round up the charge to the next largest bill. If the charge is $26.50, for example, pay $30.00, including tip.

Holiday Tipping

Workers you depend on throughout the year should all receive a holiday tip. This may include the receptionist at the gym who allows you access for those dozens of times that you forgot your membership card, to the dry cleaner who saved your silk blouse from a blueberry stain and didn't charge you extra. Twenty dollars is always a generous, standard tip—depending on the amount of regular service you receive.

Newspaper delivery boy

Between ten and fifteen dollars will make your delivery boy think twice before throwing your paper in the sprinkler.

Apartment employees

When one moves into a new building, one should check with the real estate agent regarding the standard tipping amount, since every building varies.

Child's teacher

Some families give their children's teacher a cash tip, though this is not customary. Teachers mostly receive gifts from their students. The most clever presents are gifts that the teacher could use. Ask your child what his teacher's interests are. If his teacher loves tea, a gift basket of teas would be useful. A sports fanatic? Tickets for a game, or a sports almanac. Gift certificates are always appreciated and a dependable gift.

Travel

Hotels

The bellhop

When you arrive at a nicer hotel, a bellhop typically carries your luggage. Even if you are accustomed to carrying your own bags or have luggage with those convenient wheels on them, a bellhop is more than just a hotel employee who is in better shape than the rest of the staff. He can assist and accommodate your needs for a more enjoyable stay. The standard tip for his service is five dollars, and most of them expect a tip any time they take your bags or offer you a service. Never go to a hotel without some extra bills. If you don't have any smaller change, ask the bellhop to change a larger bill at the desk. Also, asking a bellhop to use his cart is akin to asking a limo driver if you could drive his vehicle.

The chambermaid

The chambermaid is not a personal maid, so be sure to keep your clothes and belongings tidy. Tip the chambermaid one dollar per service or five dollars a day, or you may want to just give her a larger tip at the end of your stay.

The doorman

He should be tipped one dollar if he assists with your bags or help hail a cab.

Hotel waiters

The headwaiter should be tipped accordingly if he offers you any special services or you foresee any throughout the week. The waiter receives 5 percent of the check when there is a service charge, and 15 to 20 percent when there isn't.

Room service

Room service employees should also receive 15 to 20 percent of your tip in addition to the room-service charge. Any special requests, such as extra towels or a morning paper, should be awarded with a tip.

Limousines

Tip 15 to 20 percent of the bill. It's not necessary to tip airline limousines.

Airport luggage carrier

A dollar per bag.

Cruises

Before going on a cruise, travelers are usually given a tip chart. Tipping the cabin people is especially important, since most of their income is based on earnings from tips.

DO'S

1 Do be cognizant of new friends, and don't forget old ones when socializing after coming into some money.

2 Do keep in mind when and whom to tip.

3 Do tip employees of a caterer.

4 Do call the salon first to inquire about appropriate tips.

5 Do check with your real estate agent or other people in your apartment building on an appropriate amount to tip management.

DON'TS

(1) Don't talk about how much money you have.

(2) Don't use your financial status for social gain.

(3) Don't boast about your wins in the stock market.

(4) Don't feel obliged to quickly leave a cab after you've paid the fare.

(5) Don't go to a hotel without having some extra bills on hand.

(6) Don't feel obliged to tip extravagantly during the holidays when you are struggling financially.

FINANCIAL MATTERS QUIZ

If you come into an exorbitant amount of money, it's advisable to:
- A. Take a sensible approach, possibly investing the money.
- B. Have fun, it's the twenty-first century.
- C. Give it to charities for tax purposes.
- D. Quit your job.

ANSWER: A

If you receive a great stock tip:
- A. Tell your friends.
- B. Only tell close friends.
- C. Share with family members only.
- D. It's best to keep it to yourself.

ANSWER: D

The standard amount for most mandatory tips is:
- A. 10 percent.
- B. 15 to 20 percent.
- C. 20 to 25 percent.
- D. Whatever you feel is deserved.

ANSWER: B

Caterers should be typically tipped:
- A. 20 percent.
- B. 15 percent.
- C. 10 percent.
- D. Nothing.

ANSWER: D

A tip at a hair salon that shows your appreciation is:
- A. 15 percent.
- B. 20 percent.
- C. 25 percent.
- D. Paid in cash.

ANSWER: B

If you experienced a particularly harrowing cab ride:

    A. Tip less than 10 percent.

    B. Complain to the taxi company.

    C. Don't feel obliged to tip.

    D. Any of the above.

ANSWER: D

At a club where members are billed for the greens fee,

    A. The member should pay the caddies.

    B. The member and guest should pay the caddies.

    C. The guest should pay both caddies.

    D. A caddie does not need to be tipped.

ANSWER: C

During the holidays, you should tip:

    A. Workers whom you depend on throughout the year.

    B. The newspaper delivery boy.

    C. Your office assistant.

    D. The mailman.

ANSWER: A

Expert Advice

Terry Savage, Financial Expert

For What It's Worth

Terry Savage is a nationally recognized financial authority and television personality. Her most recent book, The Savage Truth on Money, *was named one of the "ten best money books of the year" by Amazon.com. It has also been made into an hour-long television program airing on PBS affiliates across the country. Terry is the personal finance columnist for the* Chicago Sun-Times, *Barons Online, and a financial expert on Microsoft's MoneyCentral website. She is a regular business commentator on PBS's* Nightly Business Report *and other national programs. Terry started her career as a stockbroker and became a founding member—and first woman trader—on the Chicago Board Options Exchange. She serves on the Board of Directors of McDonald's Corporation and Pennzoil-Quaker State Company.*

Americans have always had a public fascination with money and a person's occupation, yet a private reluctance to deal with financial issues. This dichotomy is inverse from what is proper in respect to financial etiquette.

Europeans are fascinated that the first thing an American asks is "What do you do?" If someone's child is engaged, it's "What do they do for a living?" As a society, we tend to define ourselves by our careers and talk very publicly about money. In intimate relationships, the discussion of money tends to be avoided. So here you have a couple that has planned the wedding, decided where they will live, named the children, but once the issue of finances arise, they're at a loss. It is perfectly appropriate that a couple discuss their financial position with each other, especially before the long-time commitment. If one has debts, for example, and you sign a joint income tax return, you're both involved.

Money is a headline subject in the new economy. In an intimate relationship, it's almost nonexistent. We scrutinize the *Forbes* 400 list with as much intensity as our own tax forms. We count other people's money, become fascinated with someone's net worth, and form perceptions of people based on their careers. On a practical level, this information is obsolete. What directly affects your life is knowing how much credit card debt your fiancée has before the wedding and how much alimony your future spouse is paying.

A candid understanding of monetary concerns also applies between generations—it's not impolite in this context. Adult children and their older parents need to have a frank, pragmatic discussion about the state of their financial affairs—not necessarily about net worth, but whether they have made future financial arrangements, an estate plan, for example. Couples with children also need to discuss with their families who the executors should be. Similarly, parents who are getting older should speak about access to their financial records so that all parties are protected.

We are too polite, or at least too reluctant, in marriage and between generations to discuss financial issues. It's ironic, then, that when the subject is other people's money, suddenly it's an open forum. It's absolutely rude to ask an acquaintance about his salary, bonuses, and stock options. It's equally rude to brag about them. There are those who measure others by their commitments. It's great to see what contributions a person makes—whether it be the person who raises children, paints murals in a public building, or volunteers at a hospital. Bottom line? Privately we should discuss money more, publicly a little more thought should be given to how we value people.

CHAPTER XVI

TRAVEL PROTOCOL

Travel Smart, Travel Safe

*W*henever you travel (no matter how near or far from home) there are always a few essentials you need to help you get to and from your destination efficiently. Take, for example, a routine trip to the market. A thwarted effort if you don't have money, your car keys, and shopping list. When traveling to a foreign country, your list of essentials becomes even longer and more important. A world traveler usually needs cash/traveler's checks, a wallet with credit cards, ID, tickets, and passport. Knowing that these necessities are close to you and in a secure place—in a handbag with a zipper or money belt, for example—you will be better able to handle the demands of travel and have more energy to enjoy your trip.

Even if you don't normally wear a watch, wear one when you travel. The expression "You're either on the train or not" is literally true when it comes to travel. Transport does not wait for the late passenger, and an entire trip can be compromised as a result of a missed flight. Always give yourself more time than needed when trying to catch a bus, train, or plane—you can never predict how long it will take to get to the station or airport with traffic and other possible setbacks such as customs or possibly having to return home for something you forgot.

Stay healthy when traveling by drinking lots of *bottled* water and eat sensible foods. Carry a travel medical kit and be sure to pack any medication that you depend on at home.

Tell someone where and when you are traveling and consider calling him to say that you've safely arrived.

How to Dress and Pack

There are some who are of the mind-set that wearing sweats and a casual jacket is suitable traveling attire because it's comfortable and doesn't wrinkle. I will begin by asking if this is how you would dress when meeting with an accountant, lawyer, or anyone else from whom you expect service. "Travel neatly, you'll be treated better," says Hal Rubenstein of *InStyle*. When I travel, I usually wear comfortable pants, maybe even blue jeans with a nice jacket, but I'm always neat—presentable enough that I would feel appropriate if I bumped into someone.

Your carry-on should include those key items that you need for your trip—tickets, money, cell phone, address book, Palm Pilot, and any papers that you need to get you to where you are going.

Packing

Before packing, check with your travel agent, a website, books, or any literature regarding the current weather of the place you are visiting so you can pack items that are suitable for that climate.

Your baggage can feel ten times as heavy as it did when you left home if you're running around trying to catch a flight or hail a cab. So when packing, if you don't think you'll use it, don't bring it. Unless you're going to a very remote place, you can always buy any item you may have accidentally left behind—a toothbrush or an extra sweater, for example. One trick is to have a toiletry bag just for traveling packed and ready to go at any time.

Automobiles

Have an outlined map or directions to where you're going before you even get into your car. If you become lost, I don't care how many men are in the car, take the initiative and pull over to the nearest rest stop to ask for directions. It will save everyone a lot of time, which is worth way more than the embarrassment.

Drivers must keep personal safety for them and their passengers foremost. This is one instance where consideration and concern for others have a considerably larger impact. Failing to be courteous behind the wheel is a liability and may have damaging, even fatal, consequences.

Avoid driving when you're tired. If you stop at a restaurant, the only beverages you should be drinking are nonalcoholic ones.

If a sudden storm hits or driving conditions become dangerous, pull to the side of the road or consider getting a hotel room until the weather lets up. Travel with a cell phone in case of personal or mechanical difficulties. A membership with AAA, whether you ever use it or not, gives you the assurance that you'll be provided for in case of an emergency.

Cruises

If you plan a cruise, don't expect to dress and be entertained in *Titanic* proportions—those days are as over as the movie's hoopla. Cruises are now more mainstream and less formal than they once were. Prepare accordingly by speaking to your travel agent or reading the brochures to have a full understanding of the types of climates and places you will be visiting and what the appropriate attire is. "You should always wear appropriate shoes, since decks tend to be slippery," says cruise expert Allegra Costa. "Usually cruise ships have different theme nights—black tie, western, or toga—so you should pack clothing suitable for the event," she adds. And pack key items that you depend on, notably motion sickness medicine.

Costa also recommends passengers take all safety drills, which are offered in the beginning of the cruises, with utmost seriousness.

Not tipping the on-board staff is a major faux pas. The cabin hands' salaries are mostly earned from tips.

Boats

If you are lucky enough to be invited on someone's private boat, you really have to roll with the punches. The accommodations are extremely tight and it's not like a hotel where you can ask the concierge for a change of room. Keep in mind that there is a captain, even if the captain is your friend Bob— you are still the passenger and must obey his direction from the helm.

Accommodations

For some, being adventurous means traveling without any plans, stumbling into a charming hotel, and serendipitously routing your holiday. However, if you take this approach on a trip to Vermont on Columbus Day weekend, that's not adventurous, it's foolish. Hotels, especially on holiday or in-season weekends, can be booked up for months in advance. Reserve rooms ahead of time through travel agents or by contacting the hotelier yourself. Hotels generally request a deposit, usually 25 percent of the rate. If the hotel cancels your reservation, it is usually obliged to pay you back double the deposit amount. If you cancel, the hotel is typically entitled to keep your deposit. Some hotels will return this money if there is enough notice and your room can be filled.

Arrival time should always be before 10:00 P.M. If you expect to arrive later, alert the hotel beforehand. All guests should be respectful of the visitors staying in neighboring rooms, and keep their voices and noise level down. If you don't like your room, say to the concierge, "I am not particularly happy with my room, could I have a room with a king-size bed as opposed to two singles?"

If the hotel made a mistake in not providing you with the services that you requested, as hard as it may be to do, you need to remain sensible. Just remember, people who enter the hotel business are some of the friendliest around, and it's their job to accommodate you.

Tipping in Foreign Countries

Foreign countries do not always follow the same tipping protocol as that of the United States. Many hotel prices, for example, include all taxes and the service charge in the bill. Such charges must be displayed outside the hotel, at the welcome desk, and in the rooms. European restaurants generally charge for meals in two ways: fixed menu or prix fixe for a listed price. In France, *à la carte* becomes pricier since each course has a separate price attached to it. Prices at cafés all vary, depending on location and the extra services available. For any menu that says *servis compris,* that means that the tip is included.

Traveling with a Friend

Traveling with another person—whether a friend, family member, or loved one—can be the supreme test for the relationship. Keep in mind that this is the person you will be attached to under challenging, foreign circumstances. Therefore, your compatibility with your travel companion must be seriously considered. Pick someone who shares your interests and has a similar lifestyle routine—for example, does she prefer visiting the sights or would she rather shop all day? It doesn't make much sense for a night person to travel with a morning person.

My sister Anne and I always travel together, probably better than some married couples. There is never any problem about finances; we know who has what covered. We basically like to do the same things—we like to shop, we like to sightsee, we like to eat at the same time. We typically plan our days the evening before, and there's always some give and take about what shops or museums we both want to visit. Some nights I may prefer to stay in and Anne is very understanding; she allows me to do what I want to do.

Traveling with Small Children

It's a nightmare. Picture the confined car ride and the never-ending chorus of "Are we there yet?" Kids and travel are a precarious combination. If they begin to get testy in public, it isn't fair to others. Whether in a restaurant or on a train, you need to remove your child from the area so you can attend to him without inconveniencing others.

Be prepared. You should always bring something—a toy, a book, crayons—that will occupy their attention, and food and drink. Kids are often finicky eaters and if you don't like plane food, they sure won't.

Be sensible. Don't plan a long day if you have doubts that they'll be able to hold up.

Cultural Differences

Use common sense, pick up on body language and facial expressions, and adapt to those of a foreign land the way you do to strangers back at home. If you are traveling where the customs are really foreign to your own, like a Middle Eastern country, women should be extremely mindful of wearing appropriate clothes. Always keep your legs covered—going for the sexy look is not the right idea here.

If you travel abroad, keep in mind that you are a representative, ambassador if you will, of your country and a guest in another. Therefore, you should strive to always make as good an impression as possible. It's always best to abide by the customs of the place in which you are traveling. Traveling on the London Underground, for instance, you may notice that no one seems to speak to one another. Therefore, screaming your day's events, or listening to a Walkman loudly, draws attention upon yourself.

When you are in doubt as to what to do in certain circumstances, ask. Your questions indicate your courtesy and attempts to be a considerate guest.

If you are concerned about the foods of that country, you may want to consider traveling with your own food. Peanut butter always works for me.

The language barrier is usually the major hindrance. Don't assume that everyone in the world speaks English. If you need to get by, whether at a restaurant or ticket office, travel with a dictionary. And, if you know a little bit of the language, it's always courteous to make an attempt. When your accent is utterly incomprehensible, ask for assistance from someone who speaks the language. Otherwise this is a great time to practice those skills you picked up from charades.

Taking Photographs

Pesky paparazzi aren't the only nuisances with a camera; tourists can be just as invasive. Museums, sacred destinations, and places that need to be protected for safety and cultural purposes are usually considered off-limits to photographs.

Ask permission before you take a photo. Though it's easy to just snap a picture of a typical street scene, you may offend people who don't want to be characterized as colorful locals.

Children should never be photographed in the Middle East, and it's advisable to not take pictures of women, since many Muslim women are in *purdah,* meaning that they are to be secluded from public observation.

Bargaining

The art of bargaining is more than just getting a souvenir at a better price. In many countries it's part of the livelihood of vendors in bazaars, flea markets, and medinas, and some sellers find it an insult if you don't participate. For those to whom bargaining does not come easily, there are a few general rules to help ensure that you don't offend the vendor and that you get the best price possible.

- Don't opt out of the bargaining and accept the first price offered. You will only confuse the seller and cheat yourself out of a fair price.
- Give yourself a figure—the highest price you'll pay for the item—so you don't become carried away with the haggling process.
- When a seller gives you an initial price, counter with about 30 percent of the seller's offer. Wait for a counteroffer and, if necessary, increase your offer by 10 percent.
- The outcome after a few more rounds of bids should be somewhere in between your original offer and the seller's original asking price.

If you are presented with an item and you're not sure bargaining is appropriate, say, "It's beautiful but I only have twenty dollars." Either you'll be shown something less expensive or the game is on.

While shopping in bazaars, you are sure to encounter some aggressive salesmen. Just say, "Sorry, I am on a budget and have little money to spend on gifts," or "I am a student with limited expenses."

Major Setbacks

As if trying to catch a flight isn't challenging enough. Just before my sister and I were about to board a plane in Belgium, she sensed that her passport was missing. With so many extra bags, magazines, and travel items to carry, along with the haste in keeping to a schedule, she'd completely forgotten where she put it. Instead of panicking, we stopped at a nearby bench and calmly went through the contents of her bag. The passport was indeed missing. So we retraced our steps. Anne went back to the newsstand where we bought some magazines—it wasn't there. She then recalled that she threw away an extra bag. We looked in the garbage, found the bag, and there was her passport! We just made the flight.

When major setbacks occur, the most important thing is to remain calm. The situation will only get worse if you act irrationally.

If Anne were to lose her passport or if it were stolen, we would have approached the airline desk first to let them know what happened. The airline will walk you through the procedures of handling a missing passport, hopefully putting you more at ease. We would have probably then taken a cab to the American embassy. A good reason to hold on to some of the country's currency before blowing it all on postcards and tchockes. It is the embassy's job to handle these situations. And, though a grave inconvenience, I'm sure things would have worked out fine in the end.

DO'S

1. Do wear a watch when traveling.
2. Do give yourself ample time when trying to make a travel schedule.
3. Do check on the weather conditions of your destination before packing.
4. Do bring comfortable rubber-soled shoes when traveling on a cruise.
5. Do alert your hotel if you will be arriving after 10:00 P.M.
6. Do strongly consider how compatible you will be before planning a trip with a companion.
7. Do make an attempt to speak the language.

DON'TS

1. Don't pack your most essential items in your suitcase.
2. Don't be embarrassed to ask for directions.
3. Don't drive when you are tired.
4. Don't assume special privileges when being a guest on someone's boat.
5. Don't plan a trip to a popular destination without making a hotel reservation beforehand.
6. Don't plan an ambitious day when traveling with kids.
7. Don't take pictures without consideration.

TRAVEL PROTOCOL QUIZ

An essential for a world traveler is:
    A. Money.
    B. Passport.
    C. Tickets.
    D. All of the above.
ANSWER: D

Before making a trip, it's in the best interest of safety to:
    A. Have a checkup.
    B. Call someone before you leave and when you arrive.
    C. Get lots of rest.
    D. Wear comfortable clothing.
ANSWER: B

Travel attire should be:
    A. Whatever is comfortable.
    B. Formal.
    C. Neat and presentable.
    D. Anything that's easy to pack.
ANSWER: C

An essential for a road trip is:
    A. Safety.
    B. Directions.
    C. Good music.
    D. A comfortable car.
ANSWER: A

If a hotel cancels your reservation:
    A. Ask for a recommendation for another hotel.
    B. Contact your travel agent immediately.
    C. Expect to receive double the deposit amount.
    D. Ask for a future discount.
ANSWER: C

If you are not pleased with your hotel room:
- A. Don't tip the bellboy.
- B. Politely ask the concierge if you can change rooms.
- C. Make reservations at another hotel.
- D. Try to make the best of it.

ANSWER: B

Tipping in foreign countries is:
- A. Usually different than that of the United States.
- B. The same as the United States.
- C. Not mandatory.
- D. Typically done by bartering.

ANSWER: A

Women traveling in a foreign country:
- A. Should only travel with men.
- B. Be assertive.
- C. Be mindful of that country's customs.
- D. Carry mace or protection with them.

ANSWER: C

When haggling, keep in mind:
- A. To not accept the first price offered.
- B. To give yourself a reserve figure.
- C. To counter a price with about 30 percent of the offer.
- D. All of the above.

ANSWER: D

Expert Advice

Chris Blackwell, Chairman of Island Outpost

Chatting It Up

Only someone with Chris Blackwell's unique background could have founded a company as innovative as Island Records. In time it became the finest small record company in the world—with an artist roster that has included U2, Tom Waits, and Melissa Etheridge—the envy of every major record company. Now, over forty years later, Blackwell has founded Palm Pictures, an audio/visual entertainment company, as well as overseeing Island Outpost, a collection of boutique hotels and resorts he has personally developed, cultivated, and nurtured since 1991.

The Island Outpost collection of hotels is unique because of Blackwell's ability to infuse each property with local traditions and culture, creating the type of hotels he himself would want to stay in. His vision of opening unique hotels and resorts in exquisite locations has expanded to include five hotels in South Beach and six resorts in the Caribbean.

For me the essence of traveling is not only found in the sights, cuisine, and obvious points of interest—what I find most stimulating is to engage in a conversation with the people of that place. Whether it is a driver, a guide—anybody. First, that's good manners and, second, it's good practice in all facets of life. You should be in the habit of talking politely with people around you. Too often when we're traveling, we allow the locals to be invisible to us. But by chatting with them, you get the feel of their life. You learn who they are and get a better sense of where they come from—thus you get a real sense of the place and people of the place that you are visiting. That's a lot more memorable than knowing where there's a good restaurant.

By making a personal connection, you may also get that insider information tailored to your specific interests that no guidebook could recommend. One example is a conversation I had with a driver when I was visiting Paris. He was playing some interesting music that I was curious about. I asked him what it was. He said it was the music from the film *Léon*. (When it came out in America, it was titled *The Professional*.) I actually went to see that film in France based on this conversation, and it is one of the best films that I have ever seen. So these kinds of friendly exchanges are something that I do all the time, and every time, I feel I become more connected and a genuine part of that place.

What could be a mundane moment then has some depth. Speaking with strangers, from any custom, comes naturally to me. I think that when you ask people to speak about themselves, they warm up, and you then also share a part of yourself. It's a closeness that is real, friendly. This is the best way to get over cultural differences, by just talking to other people.

Every Other Day Etiquette

$\mathcal{G}$ood manners are like a woman's handbag or man's wallet—you take them with you everywhere. You need to employ etiquette with every gesture and show others your courtesy in all regular places of contact—the gym, on a playing field, or with those who work for you in your home. By

doing so, you will make the most of all those regular moments, which will add up to a more enjoyable day—which is not a bad ambition.

Household Help

When you hire someone for household employment, rules need to be established at the beginning—from the simplest things such as how to answer the phone to how many days vacation the employee may receive. If you're hiring someone to clean your home, for example, take her through the house, room by room, and outline what her duties will be. You need to be patient. It can be a lot of information to remember, and very often things need to be repeated. Just keep in mind that sometimes a task needs to be done a few times before it's finally mastered.

Honesty and forthrightness regarding the job are the best approach, and the one that will lead to the most satisfactory results. Be honest about needs even if you think they're quirky. You can't expect the employee to read your mind or know instantly the particulars of how you want things done. Also, if you like your staff to look professional, you can either provide them with suitable clothing or ask them to wear a standard outfit such as black pants and white top.

It's also important to tell your employees what you don't want done (cleaning breakables or washing fine linens, for instance). And remember to ask if there is anything that he or she won't do.

I could never understand why people treat their help poorly. You are in closer contact with your household employees than you are with some friends and family. You need to be courteous and respectful of an employee who is doing his or her job. If for some reason it doesn't work out, you need to be direct about correcting the situation. You could say, "I don't think you are happy in your job." Depending on how long the employee has been with you, consider giving a severance pay. If someone were with me for over a year, I would give him or her one week's pay along with an innocuous recommendation. For example, "John managed to come to work on time."

The Baby-sitter

A baby-sitter shouldn't be hired out of convenience, desperation, or for his skill in making a microwave pizza, but rather based on whether he can cope in an emergency and will be a reliable and positive influence on your children.

Age is less of a distinguishing factor than the sitter's experience with children. A twelve- or thirteen-year-old, for example, who cares for younger brothers or sisters is more desirable than a seventeen-year-old who can't relate to children.

Write down specific instructions for the sitter, such as the children's routines, feeding, and time for bed. Naturally leave your number and other emergency contact information. It's also a good idea to call in during the evening.

Your responsibility is to also let the sitter know what is available in your home (food, videos, etc.). If the sitter is staying for dinner, a meal must be provided. Also let him or her know when you will be arriving home and abide by this time. Pay your sitter the rate standard in your community.

Automated Teller Machines

One might tend to feel a little intimidated accessing money in public, especially when there are swarms of people around. Punching in your password and withdrawing cash in open view doesn't ever seem quite safe to me. Every courtesy should be given to the person accessing an ATM. Always leave enough space between you and him so he can feel private and secure. Follow the line along the circumference of the banister and, in smaller ATM booths, leave as much room as possible.

Foul Weather Behavior

Just because it's foul outside doesn't mean that your behavior has to be. I'm always surprised by the careless way some people handle their umbrellas—a pointy device, typically the size of a rifle—which can be treated as a weapon in the wrong hands. Just because one is in possession of this water-resistant shield does not grant her the privilege of not yielding to fellow pedestrians. Streets can be crowded enough—add umbrellas and flooded sidewalks, and they can become war grounds. However, for every offender of foul weather behavior, there are those who uphold proper manners—even on rainy days. These are the people who lift their umbrella over a smaller pedestrian and avoid opening it in a crowded space. Everyone should learn to hold umbrellas high enough so that they can see where they are walking and to opt for a size that is manageable, not something that you could shield your patio furniture with. The drenched umbrella should never be left on seats or in harm's way on public transportation. Until umbrellas come with such instructions—marketers, take note—let's all try to make rainy days a little less treacherous.

Dry Cleaners

Ever wonder why some dry cleaners deliver your clothes in those "We Love Our Customers" bags? Sending your clothes to be laundered can be messy business—while they may have gotten out the coffee stain you requested, your coat now has two missing buttons. While all policies differ, the respectable dry cleaner, the one that's been on your neighborhood block for over twenty years, understands the value of customer relations. If a dry cleaner charges you a little more but provides impeccable service, then the extra cost could be a sound investment over the cleaner that has a knack for returning your once-white shirts in soft hues of pink.

If you are trying out a new cleaner, take the time to learn their policies. Are they responsible for damaged goods? Will they replace lost buttons? Says John Mahdenssian of Madame Paulette Dry Cleaners in New York, it's also advisable to inspect each garment before you entrust it to the cleaner. If you are dissatisfied, they value your relationship and will work with you to find a reasonable solution.

Spectator Sports

Some people assume that buying a ticket to a sporting event gives them the right to do and say whatever they want as loud as they want in a public space. However, how you act on your sofa at home doesn't cut it in an arena with strangers. Orderly conduct is essential, cursing has no place in public, and alcohol intake should be kept to a limit.

If you must enter or leave your seat during a game, do so during a lull so that you won't block the vision of those seated around you. Similarly, unless other fans share your emotional frenzy of jumping up every time a play is exceptional, remain in your seat. It's also unfair to those behind you to hold your child up for the whole game so he or she can see better.

Parents and Their Child's Sporting Competitions

Ever notice how the most perfectly polite adults can turn into the most obnoxious boors at their children's sporting events? What drives this transformation, I'll never know, but it's certainly one of the worst displays of bad manners—not only because it disturbs the other spectators, but because it can have serious negative effects on the child. Such a parent, who places so much importance on winning, may be disturbed to discover that his child is sitting on the sidelines due to unsportsmanlike conduct during practice and games. Sports offer so many positives for children—health benefits, an outlet for emotions and physical urges, an ability to meet others, work as a team, and a proud sense of competition—it's no wonder that colleges are impressed by an applicant who has been involved in team sports.

Good Sportsmanship

The best athletes are not the ones who have the highest RBIs or hold the most records, they're the ones who play by the rules with courtesy—respecting their opponent and the game. Sportsmanship, like courage, is merely grace under pressure. Always follow the rules, not only to uphold proper etiquette, but for safety purposes as well. Intentionally tripping someone who is about to score the winning goal on a soccer field won't just make you look ill-equipped to handle a loss, it could also result in an injury.

Rules of sportsmanship should be obeyed off the field as well. Even a bet placed casually can result in a debt and, if you made the bet, be prepared to pay up immediately. As for cheating, even the most honest are tempted over a too-close-to-call match point. If you do practice a sleight of hand, it would be foolish to think that your opponent hasn't noticed. Though it may not be mentioned to your face, such unfavorable behavior will most likely be acknowledged privately and perhaps talked about.

All athletes need to respect the code of commonsense courtesy. Allow your partner every advantage so that she can perform to the best of her ability, without any interference from you.

It's not just how you win, but how you act in a loss. A good loser is someone who can walk away at the end of the game and realize that it was just that. A good winner doesn't bask in the glory too long.

Following are some golden rules to good sportsmanship:

- The true athlete plays the game to the best of his ability—allowing his opponent every consideration.
- Those who need to cheat or manipulate the rules can never truly win a game.
- Allowing your partner to play to his given advantage is a mark of respect for your opponent and the game.
- A good winner is mindful of his opponent's efforts.
- Accepting defeat gracefully is as exemplary as winning.

Lastly, if you're not having fun even though you may be behind, you're missing the thrill of the game.

Skiers Versus Snowboarders

I've been an avid skier all my life. What makes for a great day of skiing is friendly interaction with those with whom I share the mountain. From lift lines to lunch lines and everything in between, proper downhill ski etiquette always has safety foremost in mind. The fundamentals are: yield to fellow skiers, don't cut on the lift lines, maintain controllable speeds, and don't ski on unmarked trails. But now that snowboarders have made their presence felt in recent years, the question remains: Can the skier and snowboarder swish down the mountain together with the same enjoyment? We're back to the valued concept of sharing. These two breeds of mountain sportsman need to be aware of each

other.

Things for skiers *and snowboarders* to keep in mind:

- Ski and board on trails that match your level, preventing any out-of-control disasters.
- When departing a chair lift, be attentive and follow all signs.
- Whenever possible, ski and board in a group.
- Be careful of when and where you stop.
- Avoid blind areas.
- Help skiers and boarders who need assistance.
- Honor the beginner skier or boarder who needs more space.

Gym Etiquette

For some reason, I always encounter members at my gym who could stand to give their manners a little workout. For starters, members of a gym need to uphold the rules of their club. A big one is how much time is spent on a machine—always be mindful of how long you are exercising on a machine and that there are probably others waiting to use the equipment. Always wipe the machine with a towel. How would you like to sit in someone else's sweat?

If you are waiting to use a piece of equipment, and you quickly leave for a drink of water or to use the rest room, tell the person behind you in line that you will be coming back so they are aware that you are waiting. If someone sneaks on ahead of you, you should say, "I believe I was here before you." Also, you can't claim a machine by putting a towel or bottled water next to it. If you do use a machine and move onto a new one with no intention of coming back, don't leave your sweaty towel behind for someone else to pick up—that's disgusting.

While the stud who can bench-press hundreds of pounds may be truly impressive, his awesome strength is quickly disregarded when he leaves the weights on the machine. For someone as weak as I, it would be an entire workout—and potential hazard—if I were to remove those weights. Therefore, always remove all weights from a machine after you use it. Also, avoid telling others that they are using equipment improperly.

Keep in mind that a gym is a public place so constant chatter may annoy other members, especially during an exercise class. Save your chatting until you've finished your exercise session.

Never bring young children to the gym unless the gym has a baby-sitting service. A gym is not a playground. It's an extremely dangerous place for a young child.

Cell phone use in a gym can be disruptive to other members. Keep in mind that everyone's exercise routines vary. Hearing someone discuss his wild evening out, as interesting as the conquests may be, could interfere with someone's workout. Most gyms do not even allow cell phone use in workout areas.

If you do not like the choice of music or what's playing on the television, ask those working out around you first if they would mind if you request a change. Otherwise, bear with it or bring a Walkman.

Also, avoid arriving late to an exercise class. Notably during a yoga class, when practitioners are finding their inner calmness, a noisy late entrance can really disrupt the mood.

In the locker room, put products back where they belong, throw towels in designated bins, and don't assume that someone will pick up after you. Locker room attendants are not paid to be your personal maid service. Leave a shower exactly the way you found it. Don't leave behind any shampoo bottles or extra towels. In a sauna or steam room, don't lie down if there is only enough room for another member to sit. Be careful not to monopolize mirror space, hair dryers, or other accessories that are for every member's use. Be respectful of other people's belongings and personal space in a cramped locker room. And anyone naked always has the right of way!

Smoking

"You've come a long way baby"—that is, in respect to the nonsmoker's right to fresh clean air. Go back to pre-WWII when Paul Henried lit Bette Davis's cigarette in *Now, Voyager,* and a whole generation swooned. Smoking was really glamorous back then: It seemed that all films of that period had a cause to light up.

Now that laws give the nonsmoker more rights than the smoker, the once-rhetorical question "Do you mind if I smoke?" is a requirement, not a polite gesture. Smokers should be accustomed to having a cigarette only in designated smoking zones so as not to inconvenience others. However, smokers should not submit to the righteous harangue of a smugly superior nonsmoker if the smoker is in a legally permitted place.

Treating Panhandlers

Some people feel that it is a humanitarian gesture to give a panhandler money. For others, like myself, you may feel you are feeding into a larger social problem. This money could be going toward alcohol, drugs—you never really know. It's better to give food but you should do so only if you feel comfortable. It's commendable to help those less fortunate. If you feel compelled to do so, make a donation to a charity of your choice that can ensure your funds are properly spent.

Birthdays

It's that one day of the year especially designed for you. All of us choose to spend our birthdays differently. Some people entertain lavishly while others may just assume that it is any other day. Regardless, it is always thoughtful to acknowledge the birthdays of those closest to you. Use your Palm Pilot or yearly calendar to record the birthdays of those most important to you if you have a knack for forgetting particular dates. Celebrating someone's birthday doesn't have to be as elaborate as throwing a lavish party or sending an expensive gift. It can be as simple as a phone call or sending an e-mail.

If someone close to you hints that he would like a fuss made over his birthday, try to be a good friend and oblige his request—within reason. However, the person who expects everyone to celebrate his birthday in grandeur should expect to reciprocate with those who honored his request.

Gift Giving

Giving a box of chocolates to someone who is chronically dieting or a pedicure to someone who is insecure about the appearance of her feet is insensitive. Remember the person to whom you're giving. The gift is for her enjoyment, not yours.

From family members to casual acquaintances, successful gift giving means picking up on that person's characteristic likes and dislikes. A clotheshorse will always appreciate the latest trend in an unexpected color. While money may seem impersonal, it's just the right thing for a couple starting out together or an elderly woman who recently lost her spouse. Gift certificates for a record store or the recipient's favorite shop is a guarantee that she will receive something that she wants.

If you do receive a gift that you have no use for, don't show your displeasure to the giver. This is one of those times where a little white lie is acceptable. Find something optimistic to say about the present, such as: "These ceramic figurines remind me of my aunt Edna's mantel. Thank you so much." And then make room for more storage space.

DO'S

1. Do be patient with new employees who work in your home.
2. Do go over your garments with the dry cleaner beforehand.
3. Do behave with courtesy at a sporting event.
4. Do smoke only in a place that legally permits you to do so.
5. Do be appreciative when receiving a gift, even though you may have no use for it.

DON'TS

① Don't use your umbrella as a weapon.
② Don't hover over a person at an ATM.
③ Don't pressure your kids at their sporting events.
④ Don't monopolize a machine at a health club.

EVERY OTHER DAY ETIQUETTE QUIZ

The pedestrian who should lift his umbrella to let others safely pass is:
  A. The one with the bigger umbrella.
  B. The man.
  C. The woman.
  D. The taller person.
ANSWER: D

When hiring household help:
  A. Outline your needs early on.
  B. Assume that they know their jobs.
  C. Establish rules as you go along.
  D. Show them how it should be done yourself.
ANSWER: A

The standard payment for a baby-sitter is:
  A. Ten dollars an hour.
  B. Fifteen dollars an hour.
  C. The standard rate of your community.
  D. Based on the sitter's experience.
ANSWER: C

A benefit for a child to be involved in a team sport is:
  A. Health.
  B. Being involved in teamwork.
  C. A good activity to list on his college application.
  D. All of the above.
ANSWER: D

A good winner:
  A. Is in the best shape.
  B. Is mindful of his opponent's efforts.
  C. Excels at the game.
  D. Can outsmart his opponent.

ANSWER: B

Skiers should give the right of way to:
    A. Snowboarders.
    B. Kids.
    C. Beginners.
    D. Groups.
ANSWER: C

When giving a gift, it's especially important to keep in mind:
    A. That it's the thought that counts.
    B. It should be more expensive than a gift you received.
    C. The interests and needs of the recipient.
    D. All of the above.
ANSWER: C

INDEX